6/93

ANASAZI PLACES

A niche of diverse supportive life
within the cliffs of Canyon de Chelly
is represented by the resilience of a
weather-tormented tree. Its shadow
darkly imprints an impenetrable sheer
rock wall.

In a vast land where the lithic forces of the earth's crust are seldom burdened by topsoil or vegetation, the Anasazi, "the ancient ones," created a unique Stone Age culture amid superhuman geologic formations.

Anasazi Places
The Photographic Vision of William Current

TEXT BY JEFFREY COOK

Foreword by Karen Sinsheimer

 UNIVERSITY OF TEXAS PRESS, AUSTIN

First Edition, 1992

Requests for permission to reproduce
material from this work should be sent to
Permissions, University of Texas Press,
Box 7819, Austin, Texas 78713-7819.

○∞ The paper used in this publication
meets the minimum requirements of
American National Standard for
Information Sciences—Permanence of
Paper for Printed Library Materials,
ANSI Z39.48-1984.

LIBRARY OF CONGRESS
CATALOGING-IN-PUBLICATION
DATA

Cook, Jeffrey.
    Anasazi places : the photographic
vision of William Current / text by
Jeffrey Cook ; foreword by Karen
Sinsheimer. — 1st ed.
        p.   cm.
    Includes bibliographical references
(p.   ) and index.
    ISBN 0-292-76515-0 (cloth : alk. paper)
1. Pueblo Indians—Architecture—
Pictorial works.   2. Pueblos—Pictorial
works.   3. Cliff-dwellings—Pictorial
works.   4. Current, William R.
I. Current, William R.   II. Title.
E99.P9C73   1992
779'.9978—dc20   91-35194
                                CIP

CONTENTS

The singular image of Oak Tree House in Fewkes Canyon summarizes the prototypical protective cliff house setting. Although it is ruined, there is a sense of security and well-being as one looks out into a complex world from a generous lens in the bedrock. Although it appears to be a single-family house, this compact ruin once contained more than fifty rooms and six kivas. The photographer seems to be hovering in space to provide this intimate private view.

PREFACE

Few books have made so indelible an impression on my book-filled memory as William Current's photographic essay, *Pueblo Architecture of the Southwest*. Published in 1971, its fine-grained images urged me to travel back again and again to those noble prehistoric places we now credit to the Anasazi. And as my own life has become more deeply embedded in the natural environmental grandeur of the low desert, I have become increasingly awed by the environmental fit of the Stone Age "ancient ones" in the arid high plateaus.

This explains why it has been so stimulating to engage those classic photographs of William Current for this new presentation to another generation. To discover a substantial number of Current's unpublished Anasazi photographs and to reorder their combined impact in fresh sequences have been doubly reinforcing. They have brought new perceptions, both of our Anasazi inheritance and of the photographer's artistic insights. I never met William Current in person. But I have studied his prints, and I have visited their places. I have breathed the same air, and I share his vital quest.

Our joint effort is neither an album of photographs nor a history of Anasazi architecture, neither a scientific documentation of facts nor a fiction of romance. Rather, it is a collaboration of informed environmental notes by two twentieth-century explorers, in concert with our prehistoric kindred spirits. It is a search for comprehensible environment, for recognizable human place.

My involvement in this search back through time has flowered because of the dedicated support of John Kyle, former director of the University of Texas Press, and of Karen Current Sinsheimer, once companion and wife of the photographer and now curator of photography of the Museum of Fine Art in Santa Barbara, California. Both have been generously and sensitively helpful. Many others, from emerging Navajo shaman to childhood chums, from hiking buddies to Emerson scholars, have contributed in significant but in less visible or knowing ways. Ultimately, the interpretation of conflicting concepts of Anasazi prehistory, as well as the suggestive descriptions, are my own, as the photographs are uniquely William Current's.

JEFFREY COOK
Paradise Valley, Arizona

In the light of a deepened twilight, the ghostly indentations of Anasazi rooms in the cliff of Long House rhythmically step away under a rocky drape. The eroded stone face seems unveiled by raising a stony curtain of tears, a surreal search through graphic transformation for some half-forgotten great, ancient moment.

William R. Current
SEPTEMBER 30, 1922–AUGUST 25, 1986

FOREWORD

WILLIAM R. CURRENT's first photographic journey to the Southwest came late in his thirties, but from that moment he would return again and again throughout his life to experience, as if for the first time, that magical part of the world. The power of the Anasazi aesthetic, the beauty and drama of the sites in which they chose to build their dwellings, the demanding, difficult but harshly beautiful land unfailingly drew him back. To his eyes, the landscape of the Southwest and the architecture of the "ancient ones" were ever new and renewing. From the thousands of images William Current made, in a career that spanned nearly five decades, his images of the Southwest are among his most compelling.

William Current's photographic career dates to his teenage years, when he taught himself to use his grandfather's 5 × 7 view camera. From that time, photography became the focus around which his life revolved, though, as with most lives, there would be divergences. World War II began, refocusing both national and individual goals, including those of then nineteen-year-old Current. In 1942 he found himself in combat in the European Theatre and North Africa, and for the next three and one-half years his life focused on survival amid dreams of war's end. A few years into the war, he suffered a direct hit in his shoulder but was sent back into combat. In 1945, having lain entrapped in a field in France for nearly three days, his feet frozen, he was rescued and taken to a field hospital. Lines were drawn on his limbs to indicate amputation, but the operation was delayed because of continuous battlefield emergencies. Days passed. Finally the surgeon came around to have a look at his feet, before surgery, and said, "It looks like some of the feeling may come back . . . you'll never walk again, but let's wait and see." Feeling slowly (painfully) did return and Current willed himself to walk again, on toes that remained locked and inflexible the rest of his life.

Returned to the United States and reclassified as a photographer, he served out his duty in New York City. There in the city where Jackson Pollock was scripting (in oil) a new chapter of modern art, a young actor named Marlon Brando played to rave reviews in *A Streetcar Named Desire,* and a transplanted Hungarian photographer, Andre Kertész, roamed his city to record its essence, William Current became a lifelong student of the photographic art.

But first came the necessity of repairing a broken body, this time his shoulder and chest where multiple pieces of shrapnel still lodged. Current returned to his native California and spent a year and a half in the hospital enduring twenty-two surgeries and constant pain. Finally able to get out of the hospital and on with life, he enrolled in the Los Angeles Art Center of Design to begin formalized training in photography. But for William Current the classroom came too late in life. Later he simply said, "I felt like an old man." He was twenty-six.

He moved to Laguna Beach, then a sleepy coastal town not unlike a village on the Riviera. Accessible only by the two-lane Pacific Coast Highway or a curving, narrow road through the sycamore-dotted Laguna Canyon, Laguna Beach became his haven. A man of intense individuality, he pursued a "photographic education" on his own terms—by seeking out photographers he most admired and testing and trying out tools, materials, and techniques through solitary explorations in the darkroom and the field. He began a lifelong dialogue with Will Connell, a teacher at the Art Center, and slowly built a close association with the urbane, sophisticated Paul Outerbridge, who then resided in Laguna. Outerbridge encouraged new approaches in portraiture, but he influenced Current even more profoundly with his intellectual and aesthetic approaches to photography as a fine art.

Current's other favored companions and teachers were books. Always seeking to learn more, throughout his life he checked out ten or more library books weekly, on widely varying subjects, and read technical catalogs as avidly as others read mysteries or novels.

In these formative years, architecture became a major photographic interest. Spanish colonial buildings prevalent throughout Southern California were a favorite subject, and that body of work caught the attention of the editor of *Architectural Forum*. Current received several commissions to photograph architecture on the West Coast. But the landscape, too, evolved as important subject matter. He roamed the rolling hills of Laguna Canyon with a variety of cameras, learning, testing, photographing the surrounds.

In 1959, a restless William Current, now skilled but always searching to know more, moved to New Mexico seeking broader photographic horizons in those magnificent, cloud-studded skies. For Current, personally, the Southwest years were a period of turmoil and unhappiness; artistically, they brought a maturity of vision and expression. He produced several groups of prints in series—New Mexico trees, mountains, adobe architecture—and a particularly Zen-like group of river rocks, of which Brett Weston wrote twenty-five years later, "I remember being influenced by his underwater river rock forms!"

Current now felt ready to go to New York. He headed directly to the Museum of Modern Art where he showed his portfolio to Edward Steichen and his new, young protégé John Szarkowski. Together they chose nine photographs for the Museum of Modern Art's landmark exhibition, The Photographer and the American Landscape, and of the nineteen photographers chosen, from Jackson to Adams, O'Sullivan to Weston, the lead photograph to the show would be Current's.

Following that memorable exhibition, opening in the fall of 1963, William returned to the Southwest, "seeking origins both in nature and architecture." Now he integrated his photographic passions— architecture and landscape—as he sought to capture the complex relationship and interplay of the harsh land to the forms of a Stone Age culture. He wrote to John Szarkowski, "With all the research I've done on the subject, I have yet to find anything in the way of a book which reveals the art quality as well as architectural artistry of those archaic ruins." He applied for a Guggenheim Fellowship to continue his photographic explorations of prehistoric Indian architecture and received one. It was May 1964.

When one considers the present-day interest in and vast visitorship to the many national parks and monuments that now protect (and make accessible) these historic sites, it is difficult to re-create the novelty of this project at the time and the difficult, sometimes amusing, often frustrating situations that Current encountered. Though the Guggenheim Foundation wrote a letter explaining a "fellow's" purpose and asking for cooperation, in many cases none was given; in some cases a less than hospitable welcome awaited. In one instance, upon being showed the beautifully embossed letter from the Guggenheim, the national park "official," who sat, feet on desk, tossed it back without reading and said, "Are you from some Jewish relief organization?" In sites, such as Mesa Verde, where the sense of abandonment and solitude is so pervasive in his images, Current asked for but was denied special permission to photograph. He simply had to take repeated guided tours, given by the Park Service, lagging behind the group for as many moments as he could stray, to take his photographs. Many of the sites were not open to the public, visited only by those in scholarly pursuits. Permission to see them was unwillingly given, if granted at all. In the end, Current often resorted to the old rule of the West, "Shoot first and ask questions later."

Still other ruins were remote and difficult to reach, accessible only on foot with the aid of a Navajo guide. Carrying his own equipment, William would walk to the site, photograph as long as possible, then walk back, all in one day. Physically, those treks demanded enormous will and determination, for every step he took from the moment he walked out of the hospital in France was uncomfortable. All that he said about the arduous physical demands: "For New York critics who have used up their last tired clichés, I advocate a fifteen-mile hike through the quicksand of Canyon de Chelly; if that doesn't evoke some new epithets, then nothing will. One can still be a Jackson or O'Sullivan out West."

Beyond his own physical difficulties and the external conditions he faced, Current set demanding artistic challenges for himself. In a time of superior, large-format camera equipment, he confronted the vastness of the southwestern landscape with only two cameras—his 2 1/4″ Rolleiflexes. He had no other cameras or lenses, and he couldn't have carried them if he had. Another challenge—to compose the image in the field. None of his 2 1/4″ negatives, from which he printed the images in this book, was "cropped" in the darkroom (selecting part of the image from the whole). He enlarged each square negative to another, larger square of 10 1/2″, or he created two 10 1/2″ squares that fit together perfectly. In his individual way, he tested the limits of his technical and artistic skill, even as he stretched beyond his physical limitations throughout his life. (He would challenge students that once they learned to use one camera with one lens to its utmost they would know photography.)

Current's technically superb prints evolved from a thorough knowledge of photographic craft (he was acknowledged in the Time-Life series on photography as one of the "Great Printers"). Beyond the darkroom, he was also a fine craftsman. He loved working with his hands, and he felt reverence for tools, materials, and the integrity of their uses. He crafted beautifully precise boxes from paper and tape for his 10 1/2″ square photographs, inventive and elegant in design; he could build furniture from the simplest materials, molding them to richness. So he stood in particular awe of Anasazi architecture with its finely textured geometries of circles and squares, crafted in spectacular and dramatic settings, because he understood, in a way perhaps others before had not, what the "ancient ones" had achieved. He knew they had pushed rock, stone, and primitive hand-made tools (there was no metal) to the limit and beyond, to artistry. He felt himself in the presence of kindred spirits.

For William Current the photographic journey into the land and legacy of the Anasazi fulfilled several personal quests. He sought to photograph "the real fact," rather than symbol. He wanted neither to romanticize, nor to personalize, nor to glorify the subject matter but rather to impart essence—what is seen/not seen. "The world is a drama of opposites. When I photograph a rock I want to portray and to preserve its identity as rock—the qualities such as hardness, strata, form by which we name it and know it. In the same photograph, I seek to reveal and to discover the essence of the rock as the embodiment of forces that created it: buffeting winds, abrading rain, beating sun."

His images, in their time, were radical and exciting. The curator of photography at the Art Institute of Chicago, Hugh Edwards, wrote the photographer: "Into these photographs you have brought more than did T. H. O'Sullivan and the others and not only because you have had the advantage of their pioneering. The subjects which have been treated by others become entirely new because of you. Your respect for the entire project—demonstrated by perfections of technique which are only instruments of expression with you— enlivens my admiration for you and I am delighted we are to have the opportunity to show these photographs for the first time." The Amon Carter Museum published *Pueblo Architecture of the Southwest* with the University of Texas Press, and many of the images in that book now appear in this expanded volume.

In June 1965, William Current was one of two photographers on the West Coast (the other being Ansel Adams) invited to dinner at the White House to celebrate the first "Festival of the Arts."

Bill, as his friends knew him, could talk nonstop for hours, and often profoundly, but wrote only a few paragraphs about his work. Though not as eloquent as his art or his spoken word, the thoughts, nevertheless, reflect a man of unusual intellect, who possessed great aesthetic sensitivity and who felt reverential respect for things created— both by nature and by humans—which transcended themselves.

"On the deepest level, my photographs of the natural world seek to establish relationship with the Universe. When I am in the presence of the world's oldest living beings, the Bristle Cone Pines in the High Sierras, or when I stand where the earth and sea come together, I feel myself in touch with the stuff of creation. Those moments of connection with life in all its forms are what my photographic quest in the landscape is all about."

KAREN CURRENT SINSHEIMER

Two square photographs are made independently. Each is complete in itself; each is a selected view of a particular universe; but when placed together with a common edge, they form a panoramic image. Their singular concepts and their shares of universe are compounded. The photographer William Current has characterized the land of the Anasazi at once full and empty. Vast skies and continuous horizons in the clear dry air of the high plateaus present constantly changing patterns of light and dark in a spectacular panorama of nature with no hint of human presence. The vista is simultaneously boundless and full of intimate detail.

ANASAZI PLACES

The singular dignity of an
autonomous Anasazi structure is
reinforced by its placement on a
sheltering ledge in Canyon de Chelly.
Forceful rifts and stains on massive
sheltering cliffs dramatically suggest
the fragility of human endeavor in
confronting the overwhelming forces
of nature.

INTRODUCTION

The Anasazi

The Anasazi made architecture.

Emerging from pit houses, these prehistoric people invented an original stone architecture, evolved a new form of community that we call pueblo, and transformed stark and arid places into a supportive landscape imbued with their spirit.

The Anasazi made architecture of the land.

Like all indigenous cultures, the Anasazi evolved an architecture made of the materials of their own earth, stone, and timber. Yet in the vast exposure of their high and arid plateau, the Anasazi had the need to build more than shelter. With their designs they participated in the rhythms of a land that is itself among the boldest and most architectonic of natural landscapes. By its spirit they were inspired.

The Anasazi realized their constructions through the space of nature. In canyons and on mesa tops, on cliff edges and in caves, they built with the immediate substance of nature. The refinement of Anasazi stonework was matched by their technical command of astronomic alignments and repetitive orientations. Pueblos more than thirty miles apart may deviate less than one degree in the relationship of parts. Radiating from Chaco Canyon, the Anasazi built more than 250 miles of precision-engineered straight-lined roads that defy the terrain. With rare style and profound understanding, they populated and celebrated a land that now seems uninhabitable.

The Anasazi made memorable places within and of the land.

Within the millennia of human development these events are but a moment. Rectangular Anasazi buildings appeared above ground in A.D. 700. The great pueblos with their formal public architecture began rising around A.D. 900 and had peaked by A.D. 1140. By A.D. 1300 the Anasazi had deserted their magnificent high desert lands. When the first European explorers found the abandoned structures of the Anasazi, no explanation existed as to who had been the builders. They seemed to have vanished.

The word "Anasazi" is Navajo for "the ancient ones." It also can mean "the other ones" or even "the aliens." These ancient people lived with the land in a different way from today's inhabitants. Although the Anasazi disappeared many centuries ago, some of the timbers and many of their stone walls are still in place. Some of their ethos also remains in the land, and some of their traditions and beliefs may still be perceived in the culture of the Hopi, Zuni, and Pueblo communities along the Rio Grande.

More vital are the Anasazi lessons still visible on their ancient lands, in the physical traces of their stone ruins and in the unwritten messages of natural places transformed. Through the lens of our modern minds we can still see multiple images of their human evolution, celebrations of place in nature, cosmic connections, and an ultimate loss of paradise.

Archaeologists can argue whether the Anasazi were a tight and ethnocentric population with smoothly integrated stages of sequential development or if their evolution was punctuated by the rhythmic tides of population movements, cultural waves, climatic shifts, and ecological dynamics. The increasing evidence is of a resilient and dynamically adaptive people. But whether through the staccato prodding of discontinuous events or the gradual heightening of self-determination toward some prehistoric Omega goal, the Anasazi focused successions of generations into a conscious and vibrant directed culture.

If they were inspired by the contemporary canal-building Hohokam of the low desert, who also disappeared before the first Europeans explored the site of present-day Phoenix, or whether they had heard of the first and largest city of the pre-Columbian New World in the valley of Mexico is moot. The grids of urbane Teotihuacán had been laid out in the first century A.D. and already abandoned by A.D. 750, just as the Anasazi conceived their first pueblos. The Anasazi evolved a distinct culture of their own in this most particular environment, unlike that of any other high desert peoples.

Today the Anasazi and their built places evoke unique responses. They are the most studied and admired ancient people in the United States.

We cannot know the Anasazi from their language, their literature, their cuisine, or their costume. Yet we understand their sensitivity to the material world from the aesthetic clarity of their decorative and utilitarian arts, from their jewelry and pottery. But we know the Anasazi best from their land and its architecture.

The shape of the land is the first architecture. From this, humans build their own architecture. For the Anasazi it was an architecture of ordinary found materials, without rare woods, exotic marbles, or brilliant glazes. Their standards of construction craft ranged from the most temporary and expedient to the most confident and timeless. There are still examples of jacal construction, a kind of wattle and daub with thin walls of closely spaced vertical saplings filled and

The aromatic textured bark of a
century-old Ponderosa pine
photographically suggests native
providence. The Anasazi resettled in
the forested valley of Frijoles Canyon
around A.D. 1300 next to the year-
round streams that feed the northern
Rio Grande.

For millennia the Anasazi possessed a land so dry, so harsh, so unyielding that it was unwanted by any other peoples. Today another culture marks the land in a different way. We call it the Four Corners, where the political states of Arizona, New Mexico, Utah, and Colorado meet with their straight-lined borders.

Ultimately, the Anasazi occupied an expansive territory measuring tens of thousands of square miles. Today there are over twenty-five thousand Anasazi sites in New Mexico and at least that many in Arizona, with fewer in each of Colorado and Utah.

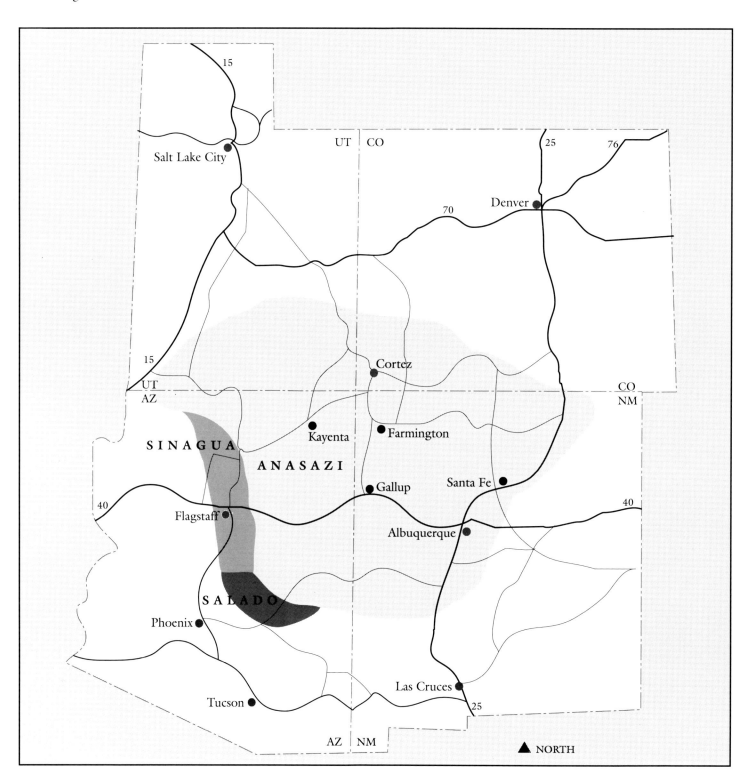

plastered with mud. There are walls stacked up of clay and stone, both crude and careful. Some are completely adobe because suitable stone was not available. Others are amalgams of mud with irregular stones. But the most memorable walls are "core and face," an alchemy of hidden cores of mud and rubble with both exposed faces of exquisitely fitted dry masonry. At Chaco Canyon the tightly laid stone fragments interlock so exactly they seem knit together by fate.

It was a stone-coursed architecture whose grand animation of geologic layers revealed the substance of the earth. Then this finely fitted craft was concealed, covered with a mud plaster finish. Anasazi architectural forms subtly resolved the universal integration of square and circle, often hidden within the folds of earth or buried within the mass of the pueblo.

It was an architecture of power and precision achieved almost without tools. There were no wheeled carts, no beasts of burden to transport stones as much as ten miles and, sometimes, great logs of cedar and ponderosa pine perhaps from over fifty miles to the place of construction. There were no metal implements to extract or to shape the pieces of rock or to hew the timber. The Stone Age architecture of the Anasazi ranks among the great refined accomplishments of prehistoric peoples. Such art has to do not only with the simplicity of the technology but also with knowing why; not only with the craft of refinement but also with the spirit that informed.

The Land

We arrive in their land today with fat bellies and soft skin, riding rubber-and-air-wheeled vehicles along rapid roadways. We come traveling in haste away from a modern culture of minutely controlled body comforts to a raw and marginal place that seems to be the end of the world, the very edge of nature. This wild and deserted territory is the center of the Anasazi world. We wonder how they survived. But they not only survived, they thrived.

Today we can still know the climatic rigors of their high plateaus and sheltered canyons, both by experience and by science. The annular rings of Anasazi timber beams preserve the rhythms and intensities of their seasons, especially the variations of moisture that limit growth in these arid places. Dendrochronology, the scientific method of tree ring dating, was developed in the Southwest during the 1920s by the astronomer Andrew E. Douglass, whose primary interest was sunspot activity and its influence on climatic patterns. Thus a scientific subfield, dendroclimatology, has become an integral part of environmental reconstruction studies for prehistoric sites. It is an intimate armature to the emerging story of the Anasazi as it has unfolded.

Perhaps the summers then may not have been quite so hot and dry. Perhaps the winters then were not so biting with cold, so lashing with wind and snow. There is evidence of the variability of their seasons, larger rhythms of weather that made shifting climatic patterns during their time. Even now sometimes the wind stops and the stillness of the air is breathtaking. Often still, the dawn is motionless. But this never was a lotus land. It was never gentle, never temperate, and never abundant except in testing human fragility. The aridity has always been harsh, the sun always brilliant, the cold always brittle, the rains always uncertain.

A thousand years ago the climate on the Colorado Plateau was similar to that of today but not the same. The constant of climate is change. In the tenth century the snow line in Utah was 1000 feet higher than today, implying average temperatures were 3°F warmer. The wet period of more abundant rain and snow between A.D. 1180 and 1215 was balanced by a period of dry decades between A.D. 1220 and 1300. The "Great Drought" in the Southwest of A.D. 1276–1299 was followed by a thirty-year wet period. But between those dramatic extremes, at that climatic pivot, the Anasazi made the decisive move of their time.

Always the Anasazi could have moved. At any stage they could have migrated to warmer, to richer, to more protective, to more provident places. But until that moment they chose to stay, to ride the nutritional and spiritual cycles of this land and to love this land with the architecture of their habitation. Our concepts of body comfort and material convenience were not the ancient standards of the Anasazi.

To scan their vast horizons of land and sky is to appreciate human suspension between the two. This is a place at the top of the world. It is at the end of the chains of the Rocky Mountains, the spine of the continent, near the Great Divide where precious headwaters originate to flow in opposite directions to the Great Oceans. It is a place at the source of air, of wind, of water and a place of origins of weather. On these dry and high plateaus the elements of nature are raw. The sun and the thunderstorm, the wind-whipped blizzard, and the blackened weather fronts are experienced as primordial.

We come traveling in haste, away from our cushioned, secure homes and familiar modern anxieties, to a place that seems to be of untempered nature. This rough and exposed province is the center of the Anasazi world, the focus of their spirit. They evidently believed that this dramatic rock-filled landscape was the correct domicile for their spirit because they cultivated it and sought to connect it to the cosmos by building permanently and decisively. They heard the fullness of its vastness.

Perhaps this land captured them and transformed them because it is so untamed, so deliberate. This ever-changing mural of natural forces is continuously interacting with the earth crust. Rock is weathered, percolated, oxidized, cemented, leached, spalled, fractured, powdered, and brutally exposed. On sun-drenched days, stone and sand reveal dramatic sparkling textures and brilliant vibrant colors. All elements are visually articulated in dramatic contrast. The distant blue-purple of mountain silhouettes, the red-orange of rocky uplifts, the slick black of desert varnish, and the whitened wisps of straw growing between loose rocks are radiant in the luminous thin air.

On cloud-filled days the land shifts into a monotone where layers of distance merge with the near into a stony continuum. Pervasive dusty textures of infinite grays test our perception of the rock-strewn land.

A mantle of snow gives yet other dimensions, obscuring subtleties and revealing crisp contrasts of sheer cliffs and ragged escarpments, of flood meadows and rock tumbles. In the sharp, clean air one can easily see landmarks fifty miles away. One can see several days of travel into the future. One can see hours and days into the unfolding of a weather event.

Threaded through this climatic and geologic revelation, this textbook of how the earth's crust was formed and folded, are the vegetative ribbons of life. Streamers of green in canyon bottoms, trees and scrub are the core of the ecological system. With roots grounded in the precious rivulets of this arid plateau, these tough growing fibers initiate the food chain. They are the vigorous lifelines that weave the skein of human support.

In three-dimensional rivers of sustenance, variegated greens of trees change to brilliant yellows as fall transforms cottonwood leaves. On upper slopes, evergreen forests thrive on uneven and seasonal rains, holding the water in the soil and stubbornly feeding headwaters. Farther up, the piñon and sage make irregular vegetative spots of organic persistence.

This inconsistent union of geology and vegetation provides diverse niches of nature, with gradations, overlaps, and complements. The earliest Anasazi understood the sparse riches of these ecological diversities, which were the basis of their sustenance, informing their daily movements and directing the locations of their habitations. And in the intimate incisiveness of siting their buildings, where forms interlock with the subtleties of the land, the Anasazi understood and expanded their wisdom of natural place.

The Anasazi surely were inspired by their spirited and muscular land. Each settlement tells us how they read the rock-filled mantle of

A sparkling river ripples through rich
sediment supporting a brilliant
ribbon of trees—all guarded by
somber cliffs, stained and coarse.
This hospitable setting for Anasazi
settlements in Canyon de Chelly is
simultaneously a matrix of natural
energies radiating in all directions
and a calm and joyful place.

the earth surface and how they found its spirits. Each place is its own story of poetic adaption by these perceptive people. Each settlement is observatory and retreat, each a peaceful and resilient bastion at the edge of a provocative and resistant natural world.

Each settlement is resolved into an architectural statement of unpretentious being. We find no ceremonial entry points, no portals of acceptance, no gateways, no pivotal focuses, and no rhythmic avenues. We perceive none of the obvious marks of approach, of progressive transformation, of class-conscious distinction, or of ceremonial accretion. Rather, the moment of arrival was continuous, and it was of the present. Existence was prescience, not promise. The future had already unfolded. The Anasazi possessed their world uncompromised, with an appreciative sense of the continuous present and an ordered understanding of being that was seamless.

The Abandonment

The legends of the Navajo tell of the talents and fortunes of the Anasazi, of how those ancient ones sought and developed the knowledge of the gods and how eventually those ancient people became arrogant and misused their power. Then the gods became disillusioned and took away the rain and sent them out of their land. Those Anasazi who practiced the dark ways and the black arts were sent out into the desert wilderness to die. The innocent Anasazi were led in another direction by a dreamer to the watered lands beside the Rio Grande. There they settled and evolved into a series of tribes we know today as the Pueblo Indians.

The Navajo legend is reinforced by the hypotheses of anthropologists. But there is no simple explanation for the Anasazi exodus. The Anasazi are respected as an egalitarian people since there is no evidence of elitist housing or of vocational specialization or of any hierarchy in burial patterns. Each person was parent and provider, farmer and hunter. Every Anasazi was an architect and a builder. The Anasazi are also appreciated as a peaceful people through millennia, with only isolated and unexplained hints of violence in some of the very last abandoned cliff villages of Mesa Verde.

Changes of climate and thus of the carrying capacity of the land had happened before the famous thirteenth-century drought that is often identified as the cause of their abandonment of the plateaus. Tree-ring history marks a prolonged drought between A.D. 1276 and 1299 that corresponds with the great Anasazi exodus. However, the same dendroclimatology shows six other droughts of greater severity between A.D. 500 and 1300. The evidence suggests that, previously, in times of ecological stress, the Anasazi adapted by diet change and by population movement—to other parts of the plateaus or southward to the basin and range identified with the Mogollon, Salado, and Hohokam peoples. Later, it appears, the Anasazi populations moved back. Peaks of construction activity in one location were matched by cycles of diminished activity in another in an organic ebb and flow.

Yet, within Chaco Canyon, one can simplemindedly count the massive ecological price of the Anasazi's labor-intensive settlements and timber-extravagant construction. For instance, the domelike roof construction of kiva L in Pueblo Bonito required as many as 350 pine timbers in fourteen layers for its earth-covered cribwork. That could represent 350 substantial trees cut down with sharpened stone and carried from as far as thirty-eight miles away, since Chaco Canyon early lost its large trees, if it ever was well forested. Should one timber fail, the entire roof would have to be rebuilt, although many timbers could be reused.

Within Pueblo Bonito there were thirty-five round rooms, or kivas. Additional timbers were also required to span all the nonceremonial spaces, the living and storage rooms of every pueblo. One authority estimates that 215,000 trees were carried into Chaco Canyon to provide the floors and roofs of the Great Houses. Another proposes that up to 100,000 trees were necessary in the eleventh century alone. That would average a thousand a year, or almost three every day.

At Chaco Canyon there were six large pueblo communities, all started about the same time. Ultimately, there were more than seventy-five large Chaco-related pueblo communities, representing several hundred thousand trees felled only for construction. The removal of trees from stream valleys and hillsides could have had disastrous results, locally and regionally. Erosion could steal the soil. The effect on microclimate, year-round water, and wild animals for hunting could be devastating, aside from the loss of trees for further construction or even for firewood. Could such an obvious lesson not have been learned by the indigenous Anasazi, as it has been fatally missed by countless disappeared cultures, from the times of human beginnings to today?

Chaco Canyon was abandoned just as Chartres Cathedral was completed.

The Pueblo

The evolution of the pueblo was the distinctive architectural achievement of the Anasazi. Roofed by log beams with decks of sapling and clay, these megastructures were multifunctional. Within the many articulated cells of a single building were accommodations for day-to-day life, for the storage of wealth in the primary form of food, and for the social and spiritual activities that ultimately shelter and succor any society. Thus, the pueblo was not only an impressive architectural unit but also a confirmation of land-planning philosophy and community responsibility, a concretization of culture.

We do not know what the Anasazi called their invention. Our word "pueblo" is borrowed from the Spanish, meaning both a people and a village or a town. Architecturally, it is defined as one or more flat-roofed multistory structures of adobe or stone arranged in terraces and housing a number of families. As a formal design for community, it is the opposite of an isolated villa or suburban house, which is separated both physically and socially from the fabric of society. As a social design of community, "pueblo" also means more than town. The Anasazi concept of urban architecture grew from their belief in the human condition as a mutual social support system.

Although a "unit pueblo" may be quite small, perhaps only several rooms accommodating a few families, the major Anasazi pueblos now in ruins often consisted of deliberate compositions of over one hundred rooms. By our modern definitions, we see them as urban villages or miniature cities. But in the autonomy of their architectural design, and through our understanding of their complete political independence, we might conceive of them as city-states or as single-structure nations. And through our appreciation of the complete integration of every person and process accommodated like a complex extended family within a single organic design, we may call them Great Houses. If some of these Great Houses were not occupied continuously or by large populations, as recent evidence suggests, but were celebratory or ceremonial pueblos, their importance as evidence of a mature regional culture is enhanced.

The pueblo as a preplanned architectural urban unit emerged as the revolutionary phase in the evolution of Anasazi development. It initiated the climax period of their culture. The earliest ancestors on this land go back several thousand years. The earliest Anasazi stage, known as Basket Maker I, describes wandering hunters and gatherers without fixed residences. They used spears for hunting and digging sticks to plant corn or squash. They did not use bows and arrows as did their neighbors to the south but used snares to catch rabbits and other small game.

The earliest Anasazi settlements with fixed sites are known as Basket Maker II (300 B.C.–A.D. 450) and include cave and rock shelters. There were a few small open villages with shallow pit houses, partly underground single-room lodges with their floor below grade and roofs of brush and mud. Some subterranean houses are at least 2,500 years old. Lacking the pottery already known in the south, the Anasazi stored food in rock-lined pits called cists and in large baskets.

By Basket Maker III (A.D. 450–750), weaving and pottery had been introduced and the round-roomed ceremonial structures we call kivas made their appearance. The pit houses were now deeper and more substantially built. The villages were larger. The diet was enriched when bean cultivation was brought in. Cotton was introduced toward the end of the period, and the coiling technique of making pots became common. But the wheel was never known.

It was during the Pueblo period (A.D. 750–900) that the Anasazi emerged as a distinctive and even revolutionary culture. They evolved the first pueblos by moving from pit house clusters to surface structures of rectangular contiguous rooms that formed larger villages. The enlarged social unit became the architectural unit—a composition of rectangular stone cells assembled behind sunken circular ceremonial kivas. These were linked by the plazas and terraces and sheltered by ramadas, or shade roofs, where daily life was conducted outdoors.

The vertical layering of functions also symbolized the realms. The circular underground kivas were sacred and private; the rectangular cells of small rooms and storage were stacked aboveground and to the rear, and the hardened earth of the plaza was the middle ground, providing the outdoor community place of daily life in the sun.

This essay of word and picture celebrates place making during the maturity of this architectural and urban cultural invention: during Pueblo II (A.D. 900–1125), when large multistoried communities were built, and during Pueblo III (A.D. 1125–1300), when variants of the new architecture were built in an expanded territory. The dispersion of the Anasazi during Pueblo IV (A.D. 1300–1600) into new landscapes still involved large and compact new communities, but with a decline in technical quality and a cultural diffusion with other peoples. Thereafter, the Anasazi disappeared as an identifiable culture.

The Images

William Current's photographic images were made in the late 1960s when there were still only fragments of our present incomplete knowledge of the Anasazi, and when both the access and the appreciation of their remains were very uneven. Yet, Current continues the fascination and documentation of these abandoned sites since their rediscovery in the late nineteenth century. The first published plans of pueblo ruins in Chaco Canyon had the careful verbal descriptions of First Lt. James H. Simpson of the Army Topographical Engineers in 1849 who also described Anasazi ruins in Canyon de Chelly.

John Wesley Powell described prehistoric ruins in his accurate accounts of explorations in 1869 and 1871–1872 of the rivers of the Southwest, including the Colorado that runs through the Grand Canyon. These were followed by the 1873 U.S. Corps of Engineers Wheeler Survey reports, which included a photograph of White House in Canyon de Chelly, with an account of the ruin. William H. Jackson was assigned in 1874 by the federal government to photograph ruins at Mesa Verde for a report. His memorable drawing reconstructing Pueblo Bonito in Chaco Canyon and his map of the site date from 1877. Although none of his more than four hundred exposures taken there with a cumbersome 8″ × 10″ camera could be developed, he later earned the nickname of "the pioneer photographer." Other early photographers, whose documentations were also primarily scientific, included Victor Mindeleff in 1888 and Richard Wetherill in 1896 at Chaco Canyon. But already beginning in the 1880s, it was photographs of abandoned Anasazi sites that stimulated the explorations of treasure hunters, scientists, and adventurers.

Today tourist cameras abound at picturesque and remote Anasazi sites. Memories of those visits and the rich projections of our imaginations are reinforced by the creative work of such artists as William Current. He has gone to the same places as other tourists and with similar curiosities. He set his tripod on the ground at normal height. He looked through the ground glass of his view lens at the same scenes we have seen with our own eyes and our own cameras. But he has captured the sentient order and grace of an ancient culture now elusive.

In a land dominated by the rich colors of nature, Current has abstracted a polychromatic landscape through a photographic tonal range from black to white. In a land hard with the crystalline rock, he has captured substance in the flicker of light on coated paper. In a land populated with ghosts of the ancient ones, he has implied an immediacy of human intervention as though the inhabitants had just left. In a land vast with brilliant light and dark, he has expressed the patterns of growing fibers and crisp granules in subtle ranges of gray that invite human touch. People seem always present but are never seen.

Using the neutrality of a square format, William Current has choreographed the dynamics of changing skies and dramatic earth forms. There are neither fish-eye lenses to capture the endless horizons or to bring closure to architectural fragments nor bird's-eye vantage points to reinforce the total experience of their spatial drama. Like the Anasazi themselves, he has artistically created within the tight limits of what now seems a modest technology. Like the Anasazi, Current understood that architecture is neither plan nor façade nor their complex combination. Rather, architecture, whether of land or of building is the realization of the intimacy of surface and the definition of edges, between earth and sky, solid and void, fiber and crystal, whether wrenched by nature or wrought by humans, designed into meaning. The making of place is the recognition of the congruence of those edged surfaces and the ascription of meaning to both inert and living materials.

With artistic perception the photographer looked at each site uniquely. Some were seen frontally, from the middle of the tourist path, and pictured as familiar whole scenes. Others have been symbolized by looking in detail at a part or fragment. Yet others required that he beat his own path through brush and scraggy ravine to find that revealing vantage point, which also was the exact measure to fill his fixed normal lens. He framed the view on the spot, composing tight saturated images that defied cropping. Those few smaller rectangular images within these pages are the rare exceptions. His strong personal discipline was of exact composition finalized in the field, before the film was exposed. With such deceptively simple means, with great effort, and with apparently endless patience, he sought the character and intensity of each view.

What emerged from this discipline were sets of images that characterized each larger environment but without the appearance of effort or consciousness of vantage point. For instance, the moods of Canyon de Chelly are quite distinct from those of Mesa Verde. Yet, each print is so persuasive and so resolved that the photographer's art becomes almost invisible, and we as audience become involved with effortless proximity in a direct dialogue with the Anasazi and their places.

Thus, William Current caught the discrete and delicate particulars of each natural place. None is dramatized in the threatening light of impending storm or the brilliance of new snow. His images mirror environmental sensitivities in their range of daily subtleties that also characterize our appreciation of the Anasazi landscape. Every element of the physical world at every scale is in sharp focus. Beyond that he explored those universal sets of visual relationships that epitomize the quests of human enquiry: solid to void, human made to natural, chaos to order, the "will to form" from shapeless mass.

In a sense, the square photograph is the most difficult format. Although the square occasionally exists in the natural order of some crystals, our human vision usually prefers such compositions as landscapes in some aspect of a horizontal or vertical rectangle as typically seen in a 35-mm viewfinder.

William Current sometimes used filters and polarizers but no wide-angle or telephoto lenses. In a straightforward approach he perceived his landscapes directly, to shape the reality before him into a meaningful whole. Like the Anasazi who confronted their natural environment with the simplest of tools to forge their architecture, Current practiced a similar discipline with the most fundamental tools of his own time. Both compounded mastery through almost unlimited perseverance.

Current's extraordinary eye for the land was equalled by a superb printing talent. Using the standard silver emulsion Agfa papers of his time, Current produced tonal values of incredible range in each of his prints. The deepest shadows have sharp detail, while the luminous highlights maintain texture and clarity. They are the select result of methodical darkroom chemistry, rolls of tests exploring developers, and uncounted hours coaxing the potentials of a negative into a master print. His prints were mounted without mats or frames.

Like many of us, William Current did not label his photographs. He used no words or titles to suggest what we should see in his vision or how we should respond. Ultimately, his images must identify themselves in their own terms. He made hundreds of rolls of exposures. Before he died, he went through his prints of the Anasazi and their land and discarded all but about 150, which were loosely organized into sets based on location. The selection reproduced herein represents his visual summation of that heroic human dialogue with this earth. They eloquently inform our individual and collective histories.

Brittle textures of desiccation on the expansive treeless Chaco plateau are emphasized by puffy fair-weather clouds. There will be no rain for this recalcitrant land. The hint of a verdant canyon or hidden pueblos in the middle distance is uncertain.

CHACO CANYON

Chaco Wash cuts through an arid plateau in the southern half of the San Juan Basin, bounded on the east by the high country of the Continental Divide and on the west by the Chuska Mountains. Today it is in the vacant northwest quadrant of New Mexico. But Chaco Canyon with its twelve large pueblos and many medium- and smaller-sized ruins is central conceptually to understanding Anasazi culture. The spectrum of building sizes and types suggests a population concentration that flourished and built between A.D. 920 and 1120, establishing the Pueblo II period. Around A.D. 1025 there may have been three thousand people living at Chaco. Fifty years later the population had doubled to occupy four hundred sites. Chaco was the location of the great age of pueblo architecture and of the most complex of Anasazi achievements.

A three-mile stretch of Chaco Canyon at an elevation of 6,100 feet centers the Chaco Culture National Historic Park. Here are the remains of five major pueblos spaced less than a half mile apart. Each is of distinct and autonomous design. One large and singular kiva with its circular ceremonial roofed space, Casa Rinconada, is the only major structure in the canyon south of Chaco Wash.

As impressive as the grand designs of distinct pueblos is their relationship to natural setting. Cliffs, especially on the north, define a climatic microcosm that provides wind sheltering and a solar backstop during winter. At the east end, the solitary Fajada Butte stands sentinel to the opening of the valley. Peñasco Blanco, a pueblo on top of the mesa, overlooks the west end of the canyon.

On the exposed rock of the adjacent plateaus and mesas are the remains of smaller pueblos, outlying villages, and outlooks and faint traces of the radiating system of ceremonial roadways. Almost invisible is the beginning of the Great North Road that shoots northward in an undeviating line for thirty miles. When William Current photographically explored the Anasazi over a generation ago, the ancient roads, the outliers, and many other elements special to Chaco culture were unknown.

Even if this treeless emptiness once was more verdant, it was sparse at best. Creeks and canyons always collected the uncertain rain shed by barren rocks and clutched the water that sustains vegetation. At Chaco the human intervention of water harvesting and agricultural irrigation extended the diversity of foods from natural ecological

Chaco Canyon, with its many freestanding Great Houses, is in a remote part of the northwest quadrant of New Mexico. Unpaved and weather-variable roads provide restricted access to the Chaco Culture National Historical Park southwest from Nageezi. Roads are paved north from Interstate Highway 40 via the Thoreau exit and through Crownpoint, except the last twenty miles. The Anasazi pueblo at Aztec in the Four Corners area is also a national monument, but it is easily accessible.

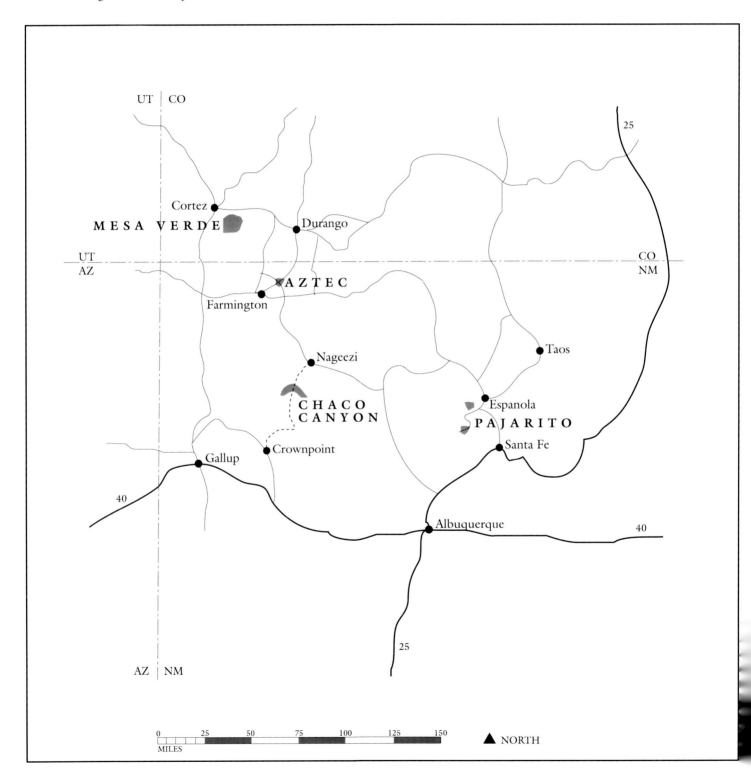

niches to add life support. But, as everywhere, the climate was inconstant. With scant resources that were also unpredictable, the Anasazi attracted no competing peoples and evolved their peaceful dialogue with a defiant land.

The classic Bonito phase around A.D. 1000 at Chaco climaxed 6,000 years of human occupation. It is named after a kind of Anasazi architectural apogee. Pueblo Bonito was an autonomous community for 200 years. It is among the first and best dated prehistoric sites in the Southwest. This great cup-shaped city facing south is hard under the sheltering north cliff. Under construction for 150 years, its protective curved rear wall ultimately rose five stories.

Pueblo Bonito is regarded as the signature masterpiece of the culture. It is the largest single building of the Anasazi and the largest prehistoric structure remaining in the United States. Covering more than three acres and built in phases, it had more than six hundred rectangular rooms, two great kivas, and many smaller kivas, or sunken round rooms. Based on the evidence of relatively few trash middens, a paucity of burials, and very few fire hearths, it is now believed that it was not occupied by large numbers on a continuous basis, although it could accommodate a population of over one thousand. Its distinctive plan form is as remarkable as the refinement of its masonry walls.

The tapered rubble-cored stone walls of Pueblo Bonito probably best exemplify our idealism about the Anasazi individual and community. Virtually every foot of every wall is different. Although specialists identify the chronology of five major wall-face patterns, each reflects a cooperative communal discipline exercised by modestly skilled but unspecialized individuals. Some of the subtle pattern shifts may even illustrate the growing craftsmanship of individuals learning by doing within their egalitarian culture. The precisely smooth surfaces interweave tabular stones and blocks, spalls and slivers, in a refined economy of coursed masonry that implies no waste. Not driven by their efficiency and not guided by our aesthetics, the patient and refined patterning of Chaco stone walls miniaturized a human ordering of the natural world.

But the stony land was less provident in supplying food. The Anasazi alliance with their land eroded just as these stone cities were completed. Abandonment began about A.D. 1125. Today deliberately unpaved and unpredictable roads to a desolate Chaco Canyon and the absence of food and shelter impose a small control on the waves of enthusiastic tourists. During the decade of the 1980s between fifty thousand and sixty thousand people visited Chaco annually.

The rhythms of fitted discrete stones flow into massive continuity. Fractured rock fragments are aligned into a new stratified order of architectural masonry at the Long Wall at Chetro Ketl. Each section of masonry bespeaks the quality of an identifiable individual whose personal craft merges congruently in a common cultural fabric.

Today our name "Chaco" stimulates imaginations and challenges insights about the very essence of the Anasazi. We use terms like Chacoan, Chaco-like, Chacoesque, and the Chaco Phenomenon to describe distinctive aspects of their prehistoric culture only now being uncovered and that seem to be focused here. For a period climaxing around A.D. 1100, Chaco exercised a kind of leadership of the entire Anasazi region, a dominance that had collapsed by 1150.

But Chaco does not have the usual physical signs of a cultural capital. Rather, the subtle balance of natural forces, the place of an egalitarian community, the webs of continuity in human activity are the organizational systems both physical and spiritual of the ruined Great Houses in Chaco Canyon. Virtually invisible is the probable importance of Chaco as part of a vast regional agricultural and religious system, as a creative center of refinement in the arts, as a center for pilgrimage or tribute, as the focus of unique technical and aesthetic accomplishments, or as the generator of an extensive trading network. These concepts of regional dominion found no direct expression of authoritative centralization in the built environment. The Anasazi maintained their sets of nearby Great Houses, each apparently peaceful and unspecialized, autonomous and noncompetitive, potentially an urban-scaled reflection of their relationships between individuals.

Only at Chaco do we have the time depth of remarkable buildings developed and occupied by many succeeding generations. As a collection of ruins, Chaco Canyon is the largest and most studied prehistoric architectural site in North America. It has often been compared to the great pre-European sites of Central and South America, especially to the previous cultural centers of present-day Mexico and Peru. But unlike Chaco, their vast physical wealth was supported by rich and extensive hinterlands. Thus, the autonomy of the Anasazi, especially the apparent remoteness of a now desolate Chaco plateau with its scant resources, reinforces the great achievement of these original and unique creations. At Chaco the Anasazi indeed developed their own complex world and evolved their most inventive architecture.

At Chaco, with the originality of its Great Houses, photographer William Current was at his most inventive in communicating the spirit of Anasazi architectural achievement. He focused on the freestanding great kiva and the two largest pueblos. Although side by side, Pueblo Bonito and Chetro Ketl have distinctive architectural plan forms. Current extracted themes and synthesized relationships from the complexity of fragments and avoided showing whole structures. He did not follow other photographers in revealing the obvious circular perfection of the kiva of Casa Rinconada or in illustrating the solar-cup plan of Pueblo Bonito comprehensively from the cliff above. His views of the most creative Anasazi architecture are sober and severely edited. His intense details are disarming, not celebratory.

The finesse of refined architecture contrasted with the pathos of lonely abandonment is a dichotomous theme of William Current's stark photographs at Chaco. Perfection is shown broken. The forlorn profiles of finely woven walls are silhouetted against a blank sky, lone fragments of architectural thought in an empty wind.

Textures of hand-placed stones and layers of deliberate walls confront the raw cliff face. The making of Pueblo Bonito is juxtaposed against its origins. Horizontal continuities of built rooms are contrasted against the vertical continuities of impenetrable rock precipice. The tight composition reveals neither sky nor horizon.

Colossal boulders tumble into a talus of stone splinters that merge into the stubborn tufts of scrubby grass in Chaco Canyon. Dimensions of time, amplitudes of hardness, and sizes of natural objects describe a bold and unlikely site for settlement.

A man-made profile emerges from a contoured rocky land. A single window marks the meeting of earth and sky. The flow of nature is ennobled by the rhythms of human creations. The photographer has framed the ancient continuities of context.

Doorways frame doorways as rooms
follow rooms into the luminous
textured distance. At Pueblo Bonito
the confident succession of simple
spaces reveals community calm.
The unaffected Anasazi concept of
interior organization was as simple as
their concept of exterior ordering
was complex.

Pueblo Bonito was built for an eternity yet broken by time. Massive walls with "core and face" masonry continuously fit pieces together. Two tiny square windows, one light, one dark, provide surveillance and illuminate the matrix of human space. Broken walls pierce the emptiness of atmospheric space.

Coursed sandstone masonry was
the artistic engine of Anasazi
architecture, never more brilliant
than at Chaco Canyon. Every piece is
a jewel of integrity within the mosaic
of a larger universe. Each part of
every wall tells of both the time and
the personality of its builder.

The vegetative patterns of the desert hillside interlock the layered masses of Peñasco Blanco in a moment that seems charged. The Anasazi surveyed the expansive horizon of their arid plateau from walls as an organic part of the slope, not inside it or on top of it.

Uncertain sizes and minor
perturbations of pattern only
reinforce the artistic logic of
crystalline small-rock masonry. Beam
ends once ground smooth are now
cylinders of fragile fiber in subtle
tonal gradations.

A time-worn pyramid of broken walls challenging the split cliff face marks the persistence of the most admired of the Great Houses. Once five stories tall, the broad-footed north walls of Pueblo Bonito have a self-buttressed taper upward.

The continuous enclosure of the
great curved wall of Pueblo Bonito
rumbles around the base to embrace
the fractured profiles of inner walls,
still threatened by the brooding cliff
behind. With detail in the blackest
shadow and faint wisps in an
uncertain sky, the photographer
paints with light.

Bright sun underlines the emptiness of the once-covered mysteries of the Great Kiva in Pueblo Bonito. A segment of the circular space with its encircling bench symbolizes its predictable geometric perfection. The regularity of niches measures the equality of the thirty-four offering repositories. Four low square platforms mark the foundations of great rubble-filled columns that supported the roof over forty-five feet in diameter.

The overwhelming monumentality of Anasazi masonry is represented in the crescendo of cylindrical spaces of the kivas at Aztec West. Two masterful square photographs hinged as one communicate in panorama the scale and complex ordering of the multistory Chaco Great House sixty miles north of Chaco Canyon. Varying patterns of masonry give mixed archaeological messages to the cultural clock. Aztec was named in the conviction that construction so substantial could only have been realized by prehistoric builders from Central America.

Abstracted from the massive
amphitheater of Pueblo Bonito's
dense north side, the exterior is now
a ghostlike façade, edges nibbled
by time, smooth plaster peeled from
the varying structure of finely fitted
stone. But the regularity of beam
pockets and the crispness of openings
reveal a geometric clarity of knowing
design.

Orderly architectural transitions in the gradations of light describe the curved walls of kivas at Aztec West. The terraced pueblo and the progression of major circular spaces step toward dense cottonwoods silhouetted by puffy clouds.

Cliffs sliced from the origins of the
earth's crust hang below the ruthless
horizon of the high desert plateau. A
luminous ribbon of life-giving water
meanders through bottom sands
of Canyon de Chelly from which
rise the eroded stumps of almost
immutable cliffs.

CANYON DE CHELLY

Canyon de Chelly (pronounced d'shay) is ninety miles due west of Chaco Canyon as the eagle flies. The name comes from the Navajo word meaning rock canyon. Located in the high plateau of northeast Arizona, elevations range from 5,500 feet on the west to 7,500 feet on the east. Its unique natural environment represents a separated center in the evolution of Anasazi culture. Present-day Canyon de Chelly National Monument is within the Navajo Nation and contains two other spectacular narrow canyons: del Muerto (from the Spanish word for death) and Monument. More remote, and much more intimate, is the Navajo Tribal Park that includes Three Turkey Ruins and requires a native guide. All these canyons contain major Anasazi remains, as well as important more recent Hopi and Navajo sites. Visitors to Canyon de Chelly already number more than a million annually.

With blazing red-walled cliffs sometimes rising a thousand feet high above the streambed, these vivid sandstone canyons have had protected bottomlands with meadows and caves for tens of thousands of years. Fertile floodplains, sandbars, quicksand, and rock beds are constantly rearranged by continuously running water and irregular floods. These narrow and deep canyons, vertical walled and flat floored, provide not just awe-inspiring scenery but exceptional microclimates, protected niches with distinct subsets of climate and natural life. For eons these well-watered canyon floors have supported ecologies that complement those of the dry climates of the evergreen rims and plateaus high above. Together they provide varied and balanced sustenance throughout the seasons for human settlement.

This unique habitat within twisting canyons ribboned with flowing water contains well over seven hundred Anasazi sites. These remains represent a microcosm of Anasazi evolution in less than twenty miles of canyons. Tree ring dates from just one site, Mummy Cave, span from A.D. 348 to 1284. Archaeological excavations at the same site extend the period of Anasazi occupation from before the birth of Christ. Elsewhere are traces of their Archaic predecessors that go back to 1000 B.C.

Although these Anasazi belonged to the Kayenta subculture, their own Canyon de Chelly habitat represented a geographically separate set of settlements that were lineally connected along the canyon floors. Primary access continues to be along the stream beds, now by four-wheeled vehicles. During rainy seasons the canyon bottoms are often

Canyon de Chelly National Monument is centered in the Navajo Nation just east of Chinle, Arizona. Although only ninety miles west from Chaco Canyon, it is more than half a day by car, and many days by foot. At Canyon de Chelly there are two distinct sets of experiences separated by the cliffs: driving or hiking around the top of the canyon and touring or hiking with a guide through the canyon bottomlands.

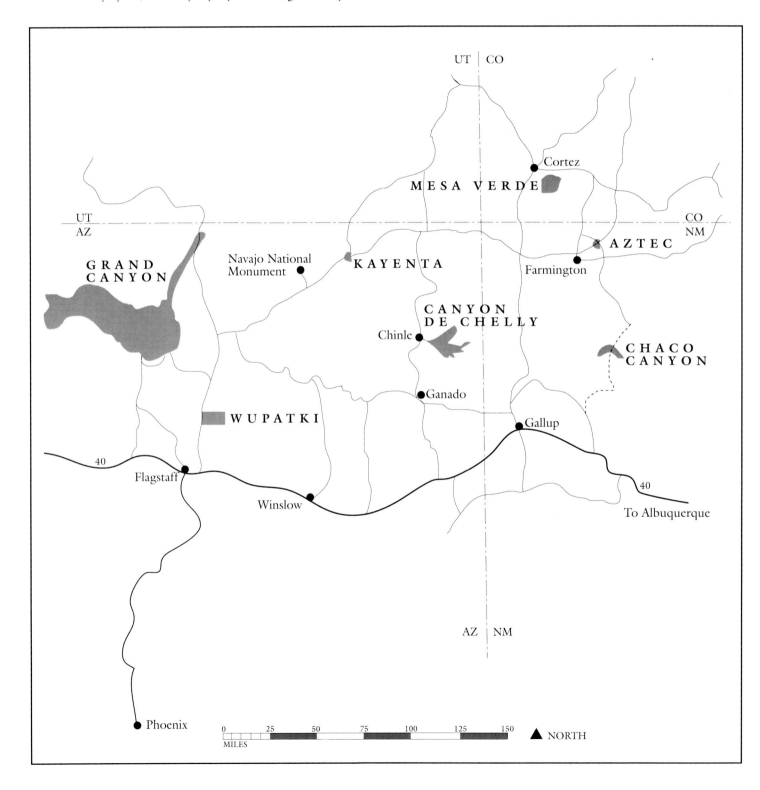

inaccessible. Today one can also view some settlements from the cliff rims. But the Anasazi passed freely both horizontally and vertically between top and bottom ecologies by cutting footholds where natural passages up the crevices were incomplete.

Perhaps six hundred to eight hundred Anasazi lived here at their peak around A.D. 1150. But all had left by around A.D. 1300. Thereafter, the abandoned apartments only occasionally sheltered wandering Hopis. Today these are among the sacred lands and sites of the Navajo, and visitors must be escorted by native guides. The spirits of the long-disappeared Anasazi must continue to be respected, and the Navajo will not enter ruins of "the ancient ones."

The Anasazi in these canyons had smaller buildings than at Chaco and only built a few large kivas. But multistory pueblos and cliff dwellings had local advantages. These construction strategies conserved precious farming space and provided safety from flash floods. Generally, the stone masonry walls were well crafted but cruder than at Chaco Canyon or Mesa Verde. Partially a reflection of the local materials, they did not achieve a local style that was distinctive or refined. Some walls may have been built by craftsmen from elsewhere. White House has some Chacoan masonry. Accurately shaped stones were carefully held in place by neat smaller spalls that minimized the importance of the thin mud mortar by carrying the compressive loads.

In Canyon de Chelly, as elsewhere, the Anasazi developed agriculture but continued hunting and gathering. Typical foods included corn, beans, squash, game, wild fruits, roots, nuts, and seeds. Cactus pads and mule deer were also eaten. Domesticated turkeys found in the Pueblo III period (A.D. 1125–1300) provided feathers as well as food.

Canyon de Chelly, with its record of human settlement for three thousand years, also contains rock art from various periods. Petroglyphs are rock-carved designs created by pecking, scratching, or abrading the patina of the surface. In contrast, pictographs are designs that are painted on the rock. Fingers or yucca leaves served as brushes. Paints consisted of finely ground minerals with a binder of water, egg white, urine, or seed oil. Rock art images from various time periods and different peoples may be side-by-side on the same site.

The vivid red color of the 200-million-year-old sandstone cliffs comes from an iron oxide, hematite, in the mineral cement that binds together the grains of sand. The shiny black "desert varnish" that dramatically streaks the canyon walls is a paper-thin manganese oxide. It is fixed from atmospheric manganese by enzymes secreted when a bacterium called metallogenium is wetted by rain and comes to life. Since desert varnish is organic and accretive, building up in intensity through time, it is a sensitive measure of environmental change as well as time. Thus, these dramatic stains are truly expressive of the global dynamics of life and earth interactions.

At Canyon de Chelly the monumental canyon itself is the grand architecture in contrast to the refined human architecture of Chaco's stone-walled Great Houses. The photographer William Current has documented Canyon de Chelly's stony textures and vibrant colors as a dramatic foil for the modest grace notes of human construction. The dominating cliffs here are both joyful and protective, in contrast to the threatening character perceived in other Anasazi lands.

The colossal scale and sliced textures of sheer cliffs provide a forceful mineral milieu for Current's photographic images. Whereas we might have only a few words for rock or stone, for cliff or canyon, people who live closer to nature often have a richer vocabulary. The photography of Current extends our sensory vocabulary about stone canyons.

In the Canyons of de Chelly and del Muerto the broken profiles of abandoned Anasazi ruins are never seen against the sky. Instead, the canyon walls themselves become an irresolute sky of unalterable stone that speaks of granular and sharp-edged protectiveness. The ancient architecture of small fitted stones is tucked onto the ledges and under the overhangs of cliff walls. Intact and unpretentious parts of empty pueblos celebrate the vitality of these human efforts. Yet their modest scale rings against the grandeur of nature's immovable crust.

The heroic quality of a human dwelling, dwarfed but not daunted, is expressed by the photographer's viewpoint. Striated blackened streaks of desert varnish underline the cliff-nested serenity of White House, known in Navajo as Kini na a kai. Pueblo construction began in A.D. 1060, with some building as late as A.D. 1275.

A powerful cliff thrusts forward
to enfold the sixty rooms and four
kivas of White House, poised on the
protective shelf of a cleft. The stucco
white wall that gave this pueblo its
name is highlighted through skillful
photography. The ruined walls in
the trees below are watched by the
magical petroglyph of a human spirit.

The simplest and most humble of architectural interventions, a stuccoed stone cell becomes a heroic moment in the restless power of a dynamic rockscape. A fragment from Ledge Ruins becomes a microcosm.

Mummy Cave in Canyon del Muerto
bursts open several hundred feet
above the streambed. The many
spaces under the great overhang are
proudly crowned by seven rooms,
including the precise three-story
tower built about A.D. 1284 by people
from the Mesa Verde area north
of the San Juan River, only to be
abandoned in fifteen years.

Current's sensuous modeling of
fibrous textures through light
enriches the stark Junction Ruin
on a ledge within a muscular cliff
that overlooks the meeting of the
canyons. Sometimes known unaffec-
tionately as Mindeleff #16, its cubic
fifteen rooms and one kiva are a
companion to nearby First Ruin.

The tonal delicacy of a sheared cliff
wall in the photographer's vision is
silhouetted by a cottonwood native
to wet bottomlands. The fringe of
finely painted Navajo animals that
gave Antelope House its name are
attributed to Dibe Yazhi—Little
Sheep—a highly respected artist
who lived here in the 1830s. Unseen
are nearby prehistoric Anasazi
pictographs.

The photographer's lens has reached into the gnarled violence of geologic formations to find a human habitation almost invisible in the frozen motion of stone. Tucked under a ledge in Tse Des Zygee Wash is the classic south-facing cliff dwelling of Three Turkey Ruin.

The massive natural architecture of
cliff walls becomes the backdrop for
the dwarfed remnants of human
presence. The side-lit ruins of
Antelope House are highlighted and
silhouetted in a dialogue of stone-
textured volumes. From above,
Navajo rabbit and lizard petroglyphs
punctuate the solemnity in comic
juxtaposition and another scale.

Within the stony arc of a protective bowl and under the continuity of a sinuous rock ledge emerges a discrete cliff village built of the same stone. The cubic volumes of Three Turkey Ruin step their masonry masses from the folds of impenetrable stone. From a difficult vantage point the photographer searches in the deep shadows for the turkey paintings that named the ruin.

Mesa Verde National Park with over 3,900 Anasazi ruins is the largest archaeology park in North America. Located in the southwestern corner of Colorado near the Four Corners, it is halfway between Denver and the Grand Canyon. Although there is great diversity in the six hundred cliff dwellings, the whole sequence of Anasazi development can be seen here in one busy national park.

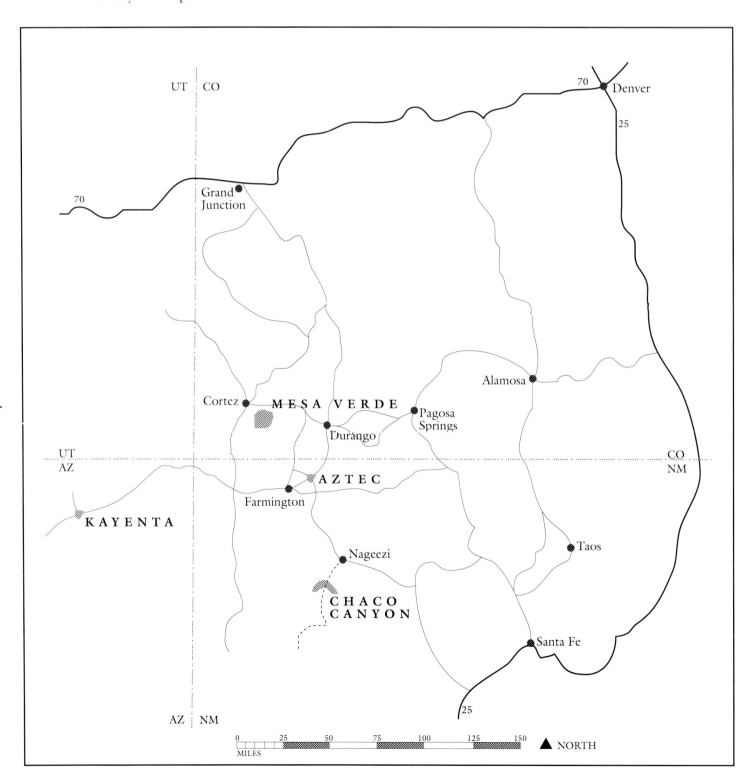

UT | CO

70 Denver

25

70

Grand
Junction

Alamosa

Cortez **M E S A V E R D E** Pagosa
Springs

Durango

UT
AZ

CO
NM

A Z T E C

Farmington

K A Y E N T A

Taos

Nageezi

**C H A C O
C A N Y O N**

Santa Fe

AZ | NM

25

0   25   50   75   100   125   150
MILES

▲ NORTH

MESA VERDE

The magnificent green tableland mountain known as Mesa Verde, named by Spanish explorers, is not quite as verdant as the name implies. It was the center for Anasazi who lived north of the San Juan River. At an elevation of 7,000 feet, its mountainous ecology of piñon and juniper plateaus, interrupted by canyons and ravines, has not changed much since the time of the first recorded Anasazi site of A.D. 608. It had a relatively long frost-free growing season of about 170 days, and the August rains and winter snows were reasonably reliable. But, as elsewhere in these high lands, winter can be severe.

Clear air has always allowed dramatic distant views. One can see as far as one hundred miles. Fertile soil and dependable water in the lower green valleys must have given the Anasazi of Mesa Verde a sense of command over a supportive and accessible land. Located almost one hundred miles north of Chaco Canyon, Mesa Verde developed a distinct branch of Anasazi culture. At its peak in the thirteenth century, the population of Mesa Verde may have been over three thousand, with many times that number living in the valley to the northwest.

Today Mesa Verde National Park in the southwest corner of Colorado contains nearly 3,900 sites of Anasazi settlement on eighty-four square miles. More than 600,000 visitors a year admire the varied and playful cliff dwellings of Mesa Verde. Yet these were the last habitations the Anasazi built here.

Mesa Verde is important because the visible archaeological record is so complete, from early earth lodges and below-grade pit houses to the single-unit pueblos of pole and adobe construction of the Pueblo I period (A.D. 750 to 900). Ultimately, pueblo complexes rose to three stories on the mesa tops. Built of thick double-coursed stone masonry of the finest craftsmanship, these community complexes of more than fifty rooms represent the Pueblo II period (A.D. 900 to 1125).

Around A.D. 1200, the population shifted back to the cliffs that had sheltered their earliest ancestors before they had taught themselves to build the simplest earth lodges. Caves and ledges became sites for the six hundred cliff dwellings of the mid thirteenth century, the largest collection of cave communities we know today. But they were occupied for a surprisingly short period. Precise dating shows construction, occupation, and abandonment in less than fifty years in most cases. It could be as short as twenty-five or thirty years, barely more than a generation. Then, like the settlements of Chaco Canyon, they were abandoned by A.D. 1300.

When rediscovered in the nineteenth century, these ruins gave the Anasazi the name of "cliff dwellers." The surveying expedition of William H. Jackson in the summer of 1874 produced a newspaper account in the *New York Tribune* on 3 November of the same year. Two years later his official report, including photography, was published. In 1893 the first scientific study, *The Cliff Dwellers of the Mesa Verde,* was published by the Swede Gustaf Nordenskiold based on his 1891 excavations. Many additional reports about the concentration of prehistoric sites at Mesa Verde encouraged serious exploratory expeditions as well as exploitive treasure hunting and flagrant vandalism.

Conscientious citizens ultimately generated protective federal legislation and the creation of Mesa Verde as a national park in 1906. It was the first national park devoted not to the preservation of natural wonders, but to the works of people. There were enough well-preserved timbers at Mesa Verde to become the critical data base for research in the late 1920s and early 1930s that established the scientific technique of tree ring dating and confirmed the Anasazi chronology. Thus, we know the dates of construction of these prehistoric sites at Mesa Verde with considerable precision. The last date of construction is A.D. 1273.

The high and broad caves protected by sandstone ledges allowed construction not just of single dwellings but also of community aggregations. Often facing south and thus open to the sun in winter, all of these late settlements had a naturally protected setting. Partly because of this protection, the walls of the late cliff dwellings at Mesa Verde are thinner than at Chaco Canyon. Flat or tabular stones also were not available. Thus, sandstones were shaped by pecking into large loaf shapes.

Square corners and window and door openings were often precisely crafted. However, within a wall only the outside vertical faces were typically made relatively straight and smooth. With single courses of chunky stone running through the wall, construction was massive with no rubble cores and scant use of mud mortar. Walls were then neatly plastered and sometimes colored or painted with symbolic designs.

The roofs of the circular rooms, or kivas, were framed much more simply and economically than at Chaco Canyon. Here a structural grille of beams might require only eight logs to span the full diameter of the plan. Large flagstones spanned between the beams and were covered with clay.

The typical Mesa Verde cliff city had no set arrangement, unlike the freestanding pueblos at Chaco Canyon with their deliberate plans. Rather, each represents an accretive process responsive to complex three-dimensional community needs. Each has rectangular and irregular storage spaces and sleeping rooms, outdoor courtyards, terraces and plazas, kivas and round towers connected by pedestrian streets. Irregular roof lines and articulated public spaces suggest animation. Cliff Palace, the largest and most picturesque ruin, had 217 rooms and 23 kivas and housed about 250 people. Functional mix and density respond organically to the natural shelter available as well as to the quality of nearby resources. Corn, squash, and bean cultivation and turkey tending were the domesticated Stone Age complements to gathering and hunting from the wild. Steps, ladders, or towers gave access to both mesa tops and canyon bottoms. The cultivated and wild produce of the two ecologies supported the habitation.

The photographs of William Current at Mesa Verde are sometimes dramatic. More often he brings a certain sense of the appropriateness and even inevitability about these geologically comfortable settlements. Included are some of the most familiar tourist views, as well as surprising details of parts that we thought we knew. Especially the overall views are presented with unfamiliar and even critical sharpness. And the vignettes and selected parts are not seen as fragments but as wholes, microcosms representing complete reality and penetrating the larger order. Photographic resolution communicates integrity of community, linking a people at home in nature.

Photographic resolution sometimes captures the animated liveliness of these deserted communities. One can project the friendly sounds of children at play, the noises of turkeys fussing in their cages, and the activities of the return of successful hunters. Sometimes the urbane stage seems set and populated, bristling with anticipation for the citizen actors to step forward. Other times the doorways yearn for a familiar shadow in their void. Spaces and façades, sometimes whole, sometimes partial, seem unready to forget their life-fulfilling purposes.

In a masterful composition of two matched exposures, Current suggests the expansive grandeur of Cliff Palace. This double framed panorama exudes the palatial quality of a richly modulated structure built by a single authority. The statement of community is highly articulate, but the solitary individual or the singular family has no expression. Even great fallen boulders near the round tower at the left are absorbed within the playful forms of the largest cliff dwelling at Mesa Verde. Above the textured surfaces of many distinct architectural elements sweeps the contrasting smooth, hard underside of the bold mesa capstone. The tiny rooms on a high secondary ledge are for safe storage.

Circles and rectangles play rhythmically with the lines of nature. Rectangular towers dance with the cliff face behind and with the open cylinders of kivas in front. With fine masonry once plastered, the three towers share a common and simple architectural vocabulary, yet each is unique, dynamically enlivening the south end of Cliff Palace.

Light and shadow create substance, elegantly modeled and articulated. The flow of pueblo forms provides a counterpoint to the geologic dynamic of the cave. Against the dark chasm of the cave is silhouetted the tallest, most imposing element of Cliff Palace. Excavator J. W. Fewkes romantically called it "speaker chief tower," implying it to be the site of major announcements, its singular elevation so addresses the community.

A slice through the textured environments of the best preserved large cliff dwelling at Mesa Verde shows its massive stone roof and deeply shadowed cave with windowed buildings. The broad public spaces are contrasted against the well-watered canyon below with its profusion of trees. Spruce Tree House was misnamed from the Douglas firs growing nearby. With 114 rooms and 8 kivas, this may have been a settlement for up to 150 people.

Mastery of the photographic medium is beautifully expressed in this wall abstraction. The composition of surface, line, and light transcend subject matter. One confronts art, in both the photographer and the builder. Soft wrinkles show through the delicate skin. Black voids of doors contrast with the tiny apertures of window or ventilator openings in the first court at Spruce Tree House. When it was occupied, the openings might have been animated by closure with loose stones and rags or remnants of turkey feather cloaks to control the icy winters, but there were no fitted doors or shutters.

In the north courtyard at Spruce Tree House the ceremonial exits from one ritual are dramatized into celebration entrances to another. The dialogue between suggestive forms is a kind of urban theater. Houses with balcony beams and with doors open to now-missing staging address the circular recess that is the roof of a kiva awaiting the ceremonies to begin.

Discrete kiva details at Spruce Tree House describe careful design inside and out. Within the cylindrical underground ceremonial chamber of the kiva, the circular recessed firepit, or hearth, is backed by a stone deflector, or draftscreen, and connected to the rectangular ventilator by a channel. The only kiva entrance was by ladder through a rectangular opening in the center of the cribbed circular roof, which was also the smoke hole. Thus, all entrances were ritualized by coming from the light of the upper world through the smoke into the lodge of the lower world.

Two windows and a T-shaped door animate a plastered wall at Balcony House. These are the only sizes of windows in Anasazi architecture. Ventilation holes like the one at floor level were even smaller. Doors, however, varied in size and shape allowing such refined forms as this proportion of the subtly tapered jambs. Doorways usually had a raised threshold with higher short side sills as handholds to step through. The wider upper part allowed loads to be carried through doorways or the passage of bulky clothing, such as turkey feather coats or ceremonial costumes and masks.

Balcony construction details show pairs of cantilevered log floor beams supporting lateral juniper poles, or stringers, with a deck of split juniper. Bark is added, and finally mud. These dramatic vignettes characterize typical Mesa Verde roof-building skills.

As if poised on air, the photographer has found the vantage position to poignantly evoke the fragile yet harmonious balance the Anasazi forged with their world. The high retaining wall at Balcony House stretches vertically across the jaws of the rugged cave. Fallen boulders are locked into the embrace of the masonry retaining walls, poising constructed and natural forms in dynamic balance. With forty-five rooms and two kivas, this was the most protectable community at Mesa Verde, although defense was not necessary.

In this image, somber of mood and dark in tonal values, the photographer has extracted detail from the shadows of the diverse space volumes inside Balcony House. A tall retaining wall tapers as it reaches for the cave roof. The sunken kiva has not had its roof restored. One- and two-story houses overlook the plaza and beyond into the canyon from their discrete positions.

A tall shallow alcove in a naturally sheltered cliff cove encouraged the multistory construction of Square Tower House. The four-story tower, actually four domestic rooms stacked above each other, seems rooted to a fault in the cliff. All the adjacent construction has fallen away to reveal in brilliant light this one defiant structure intact against the immutable bedrock.

An orderly architectural logic emerges from the size of building stones and the dimension of roof-spanning timbers. The harmonic directional vectors seem to be generated by the straight edge of the huge boulder, which extends the foundation of Square Tower as a public space of natural paving. Together they form an integrated and informed architecture, weaned by respecting the limitations of construction processes.

The photographer has conveyed the humbleness of human presence in Fewkes Canyon at Mesa Verde. At the extreme left is Fire Temple, a great kiva, and at the right of the left frame is New Fire House. Anasazi effects are incidental in the sweep of a stain-streaked geology. Without foreground and without sky, the super scale of forest, cliff face, and mesa top overwhelms the tiny buildings nested in ledges.

Human structures seem a delicate insertion in a brooding and unyielding nature. The piling up of small stones in residential building walls and the indentions of hand-toehold steps seem inconsequential in this detailed study in stone at New Fire House.

A single intact house expresses human tenacity within the chaotic natural forces of swirling layered rock formations and scattered clumps of vegetation. Other structures, both natural and constructed, seem subservient to the nobility of this lone proud house at Mesa Verde.

The rich variegation of natural textures through long scenic vistas implies the ecological diversity that supported Anasazi life in Tsegi Canyon, with its moody tones of eroded sandstone.

KAYENTA

The largest and most stunning of the Anasazi cliff communities were among the last creations of the Kayenta group of "the ancient ones." But the place-name Kayenta refers to a late-twentieth-century lineal highway settlement, not an ancient community. Located in today's Navajo National Monument within the Navajo Nation are Betatakin and Keet Seel, accessible only by a long horseback ride or a rigorous hike. Betatakin can also be seen at a distance from a scenic overlook. The third-largest cliff dwelling, Inscription House, is no longer accessible due to its fragile condition.

Betatakin is Navajo for "ledge house," referring to the steepness of its cave floor. Keet Seel is Navajo for "broken pottery." Keet Seel, with 160 rooms, is the largest Anasazi structure in Arizona. These two major cliff dwellings set in lofty vaulted red sandstone caves are among the best preserved of any abandoned Anasazi sites. Both remoteness and strategies by the National Park Service, such as access limited by reservation, have saved these sites. The heavily smoke-blackened walls and ceilings still show Anasazi housekeeping habits. Escorted by a guide, one can walk among the ancient rooms where remnants of corn, beads, baskets, and pottery still in their original locations give a sense of immediacy. The dimensions and experience of long hikes add to the intensity of projecting into the age of the Anasazi.

Kayenta is a place bounded by sacred mountains: Black Mesa to the south and Navajo Mountain to the northwest. To the northeast is Monument Valley, known to the Navajo as "Rocks Pointing Upward" for the "Sky Travelers." The San Juan River is to the north. This watershed between 7,000 and 8,000 feet in elevation is the well-creased rough terrain typical of high desert. Vast rolling horizons are articulated by eroded broad irregular canyons and high mesas covered with evergreen piñon pine and juniper.

The Kayenta Anasazi have a record of continuous habitation on the rigorous Colorado Plateau at the north side of Black Mesa from 750 B.C. to A.D. 1300, over two thousand years of cultural development in one place. Only at the end of that period did they construct their swan-song pueblo villages in the grand arched alcoves along the lushly vegetated branches of Tsegi Canyon and the more complex Navajo Canyon to the west. These were among the last of the Anasazi pueblos of the San Juan area to be occupied.

Kayenta is the name of a recent strip settlement along the highway. It is also the name of a version of Anasazi culture whose finest ruins are at Navajo National Monument, less than one hour's drive to the west.

However, Keet Seel and Betatakin, which are intact cliff dwellings, are not accessible by car. The hours of hiking required and other limits on access help to preserve their original quality.

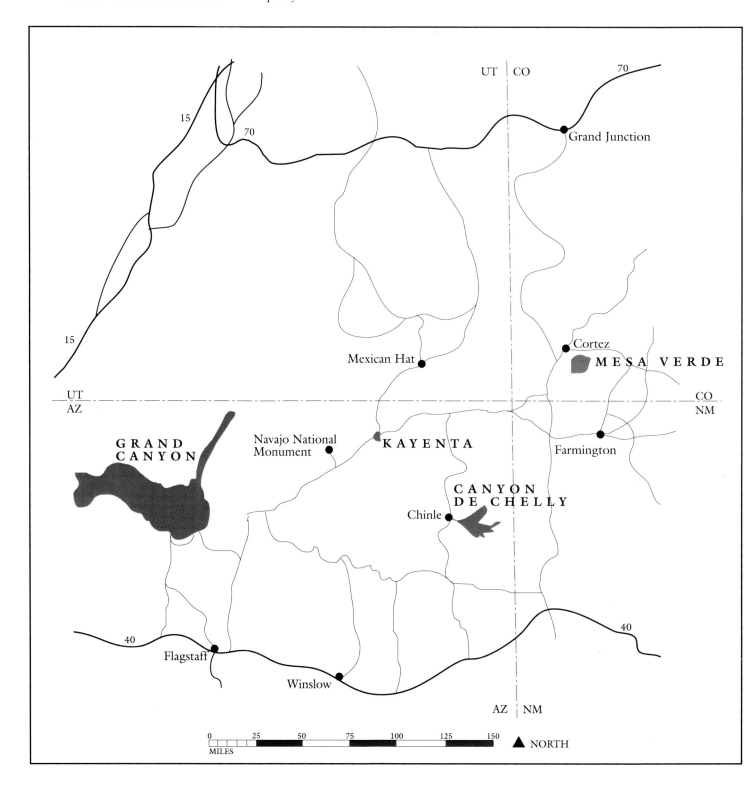

Betatakin Cave had served only as an occasional camp before four households established residency in A.D. 1267 and 1268. Population peaked at 125 people by the mid 1280s. Construction of Keet Seel began around 1250, with the major surge of building activity between 1272 and 1275. Within twenty-five years it would be abandoned. The last tree ring date is 1286 when perhaps seven hundred lived in the whole canyon. By 1300 none remained. It has been suggested that arroyo cutting destroyed the canyon fields and irrigation systems. Rather than reduce the population by partial migration, the Anasazi of Betatakin moved their entire village as a unit, settling in the Little Colorado River headwater where it is thought they became the ancestral Hopi. But the anthropological analysis of that move also illustrates the strength of Anasazi commitment to the whole community rather than splitting into smaller more easily sustained groups.

Construction within these remote caves was well sheltered. Thus, inferior masonry has survived intact. Irregularly shaped stones were set in generous quantities of adobe mortar with sloppy coursing. Then these walls were covered with mud plaster. Unusual is the use and survival of jacal. This wattle-and-daub technique uses closely spaced saplings as vertical reinforcement for thin mud walls.

The caves face south or southeast, allowing ideal solar heating in winter and self-shading in summer. These sandstone caves are huge. Betatakin is a semidome, 450 feet high, 370 feet wide, and 135 feet deep, and contains 135 rooms and one kiva. Such limestone alcoves are formed by spring sapping. Water seepage from winter snows disintegrates the rock by dissolving the calcite cement surrounding the sand grains.

The grandeur of the Kayenta landscape as captured by William Current is neither in distant horizons nor in wet stream bottoms but in bold vaulted cave-sheltered villages and their urbane details. He has found the strength of these grand arched stone hollows as natural spaces for protected settlements. He has also caught the intimate textures and sense of immediacy of their human habitation. These comfortable villages seem only vacated for the afternoon. In their complementary strengths Current's images make powerful statements about the wholeness of these human communities harmonically embraced by a massive and brawny geology.

Caught between the lush vegetation of the stream in Nitsin Canyon and the vivid blue of clear sky is the shallow shelter of Inscription House, revealed in sunshine like a kernel springing into life from the opened earth. The photographer has captured all the natural forces that shaped Anasazi lives in this prototypical settlement. The cliff dwelling glows in the luminous reflectance from its sheltering cave roof.

With a standard lens the photographer has found a viewpoint to express human scale in the forcefulness of nature. Although Betatakin embraces 135 rooms, the size pales by comparison to the weight of the magnificent monolith. A stone rainbow within the massive plateau frames this pueblo village. Its bold arc exactly facing south provides summer shade to its hearthlike cave.

Bold architectural solids reach
upward extending the vertical cliff
wall and resolving the sloped
ledges of Betatakin's cave into an
orchestration of stepped activity
stages. The sticks of ladders animate
the cliff-protected pueblo made of
the same stone. This cubic theater in
nature still awaits human actors for
the play to unfold.

A perfectly framed detail captures the essence of the Anasazi. Crude masonry walls step from toeholds chipped into the live rock of Betatakin—a delicate human insertion into a dynamic natural system. The succession of forms suggests organic growth from textured stone slopes to terraced pueblo roofs. Ladders give access to the private interiors below and imply the ultimate fragility of this human intervention within an intimidating cavern.

The humble construction materials of great architectural forms can be stones, sticks, and mud collected nearby. The elongated and unshaped stones with thick mud mortar lack the refinement of masonry at Pueblo Bonito but still made a massive and smooth wall when plastered. The close spacing of easily found saplings on the more prized log beam made a solid flat roof deck at Betatakin.

The black void through a roof hatch into the interior is framed by stones that seem to be set by a lapidary. The delicate screen wall that separates roof space from courtyard repeats the square opening. The "wattle" of vertical twigs covered by the "daub" of mud plastering is a common worldwide prehistoric construction known as "jacal."

The lush microcosm at the bottom of Betatakin Canyon contrasts with the sparseness of cliff and plateau. The print conveys the richness of the natural environment in its silvery tones of foliage, tree trunks, and cliff walls. Geological formations hint at the creation of pueblo-sized caves.

The queen of the cliff dwellings is Keet Seel, gracefully emerging from the mouth of a fecund earth. Fertile farmlands in the foreground and on the plateau above supported the pueblo. This peaceful portrait symbolizes the dramatic setting and siting of many Anasazi places where architecture was one with nature.

Two matched square frames reinforce the panoramic calm of Keet Seel within the dynamics of the natural setting. The continuity of level lines in the pueblo forms is reinforced by their horizontal masonry bedding planes. In dynamic contrast are the efflorescent trees and the sinuous cliff face. The engineering skill of the 180-foot-long masonry retaining wall unites the village as a single building. This largest cliff dwelling in the Southwest, and the best preserved, seems freshly discovered and untouched. Only the sinuous line of a ladder below gives a counterpoint hint of the twentieth century.

A carefully framed composition directs the eye into the protective cavity of Keet Seel. The weaving rhythms of human movement thread through the masonry matrix of private spaces. Rampart Street ramps up toward the west rooms of the pueblo. The great community-constructed retaining wall mediates between the architectonic planes of sloped floor ledge and textured cave ceiling.

In an exposure requiring many seconds, the photographer has brought the deepest recesses of Keet Seel into sharp focus. Crude walls meet the cave ceiling of living rock. Deep within the well-protected cliff village the once-plastered rough walls of scrap stone and wide mud mortar still stand as intimate sculpted space makers. The delicate lines of vertical sticks counterpoint the sculptured solidarity of all surfaces.

The photographer has transformed humble material into sculptural forms by skillful modeling with light, just as the Anasazi with the simplest materials and tools created significant architecture. The ancient and easy construction tradition of jacal was revived at Keet Seel with no symbolic connotations, although use had long disappeared elsewhere. This wattle and daub of mud over sticks has survived for seven centuries in the protected cave and dry air; a fragile prehistoric fragment from the beginning and the end of Anasazi time.

Complexity of urban experience is achieved with a loose grouping of humble mud-plastered walls at Keet Seel. Three pedestrian streets sculpt their way through a pueblo that once housed up to 150 people. The striated cliff wall provides a protective stone sky in a photograph of intensely tactile surfaces.

Along the northern Rio Grande the plateau west of the river and south of Espanola is called Pajarito. Near Los Alamos are many late Anasazi sites. Bandelier National Monument south of White Rock contains the cave rooms of Tyuonyi and, to the west, Long House. The ruins of Puye are in the Santa Clara Pueblo Indian Reservation to the west of Espanola.

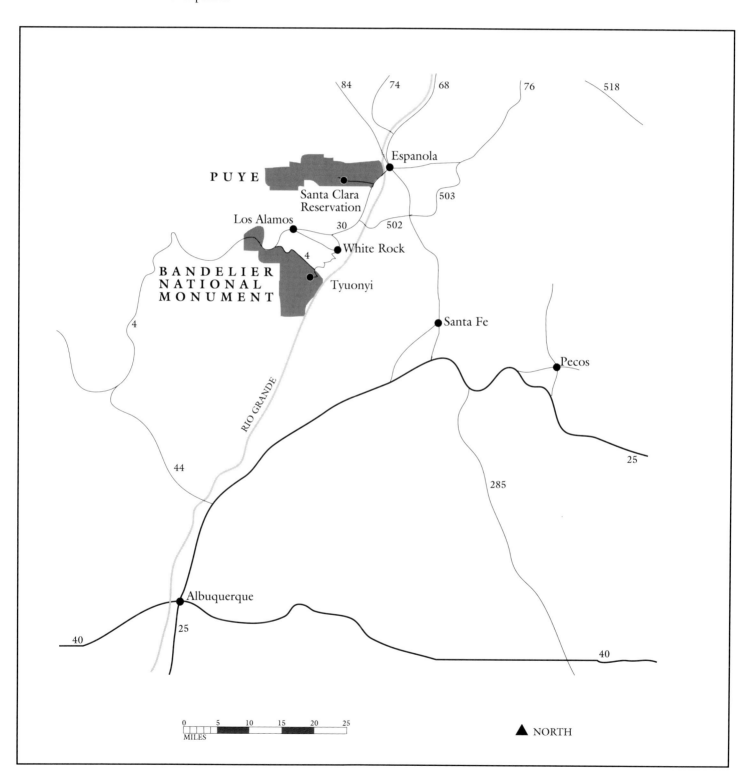

NORTHERN RIO GRANDE

The great Anasazi migrations around A.D. 1300 from Mesa Verde and Chaco Canyon were toward the forested uplands near a singular river to the east and south, to the valley of the northern Rio Grande in New Mexico. The precipitation was more dependable on the higher elevations of the Pajarito Plateau, named after its "little birds." Heavy winter snows and dramatic summer thunderstorms watered its canyon-cut mesas. But the growing season was much shorter. In spite of warm days, the cool nights stunted crops. Cool, confined canyons and narrow mesas replaced the broad arid plateaus.

There in the crystalline air of a land less grand but equally noble, the Anasazi founded new pueblo settlements of another nobility. These communities were active between A.D. 1300 and the coming of the first Europeans with the Spanish explorations, starting with Coronado in 1540. Thus, as a Pueblo IV stage, these settlements provide the link between the Stone Age culture of the ancient ones and our historic times. Today Puye is considered the ancestral home of the Santa Clara Pueblo. Tyuonyi, occupied until around A.D. 1550, is considered the root of modern Cochiti. Similar thriving pueblos of today, such as Jemez, San Ildefonso, Taos, Zia, and others, are said to have grown from fragments of the Anasazi migrations toward the Rio Grande.

The Anasazi brought with them their architectural culture of masonry pueblos, cliff dwellings, and kivas. They settled in the more intimate canyons and quiet meadows of what is now northern New Mexico. They left behind those almost endless and restless vistas at the top of the continent. If the spirit was not broken it was subdued. Large new stone-walled pueblos were developed with spacious plazas for public ceremonies and rituals, instead of the large number of kivas that distinguished their premigration pueblos. But the Anasazi continued to build designed communities of stone, and they persisted in settlements that aesthetically commanded a grand landscape. From on high they scanned the distant Sangre de Cristo Mountains to the east and savored the weather gods at play in the Rio Grande Valley.

Anasazi architecture in this new land evolved in response to a different environment. The soft stone of volcanic deposits of the Pajarito Plateau provided a poor building stone for masonry but an easy matrix for rock-cut shelter. Groups of rooms excavated in soft stone cliff faces are called "cavate" lodges. They always face the sun. Volcanic tuff was easily removed with stone or even wooden tools. In front of the excavated rooms, the floor and ceiling beams of pueblo construction were supported by notches or pockets in the cliff face. These talus pueblos like Long House were lineal, following the cliff, and could step up with usable roof terraces to three stories in height.

The Rio Grande pueblos were built in cooler and fully forested uplands, unlike the lower and drier basin lands of Chaco Canyon. In a less spectacular landscape, the Anasazi built larger and less spectacular settlements. For instance, the circular ruin of Tyuonyi (chew-ohn-yee) Pueblo on flat ground in Frijoles Canyon was next to a year-round creek named after "beans." It has more than three hundred ground-floor rooms around a central plaza. The use of second- and third-story spaces would have provided another five hundred rooms. The unexcavated pueblos of Tsankawi and Otowi had a similar size but were on mesa tops. In the number of living and storage rooms, these pueblos may have rivaled the celebrated Pueblo Bonito, but without the integrated kivas and complex plaza spaces. They were begun more than three hundred years later and conform to more elementary standards of architectural form and construction.

William Current was attracted not to the ruins of late flatland pueblos built in valley bottoms or on mesa tops, but to the haunting Anasazi cliff ruins of inner rooms at Puye and Tyuonyi. His images are dialogues between the subtle differences of cliff-bound caves and the texture of their volcanic rock; between human ecology in a ponderosa pine canyon, Tyuonyi, and in a juniper piñon one, Puye. The living rock is revealed as pocked by nature and pecked by humans. The photographer did not give us the deep turquoise of clearest skies but the somber screens of stone cliffs. He rendered the atmospheric autopsy of vacated human megastructures, of multicelled settlements interlocked with volcanic ridges where structured whole communities are now returned to a fractured state.

The ruins of Puye, in the Santa Clara Indian Reservation, are at 7,000 feet. Its one thousand rooms had a regularized mesa-top construction of multiroom blocks around a large plaza. But it is the adjacent miniature cave dwellings cut into the two terraces of vertical cliffs and their tumbling talus that challenged Current's photographic eye in mystery, distant memory, and indelible hints of forgotten times.

The ruins at Tyuonyi in Bandelier National Park are at an elevation of 6,000 feet. Here the photographer passed by the regular pueblo ruin on the canyon floor to probe the recesses of the south-facing walls of Frijoles Canyon. Equally private and haunting are his perceptions at Long House and the cliffs overlooking Tyuonyi. The carved and worn rock still seems populated by the dislocated ghosts of ancient Anasazi. The images are of the "old ones" in restless sleep.

In this grand view the lens sweeps the landscape, capturing both a minute talus house in the distance overlooking the valley and the rock detail in the foreground. Like the opened amphitheater of a stone quarry, the cliff ridge of Puye ruin almost conceals the human vestiges of cavate cliff dwellings. The Anasazi spirit once commanded the great landscape of Santa Clara at an elevation of 7,000 feet. Now the human trace has all but merged with nature.

Below: Human scratchings of permanence and fragility mark the Puye cliff face. The row of empty beam sockets denotes the roof above the second floor where the Anasazi stood to inscribe petroglyphs. Two doglike figures and a heroic man address a spiral sun; to the left is a sun face.

In the upper photograph is an image of human transience now disappeared. A wall and lintel of loose stone attempt to regularize the form of a cave doorway in an impermanent intervention.

Our tenuous hold between earth and sky is eloquently expressed in this photograph of a Puye Pueblo talus house reconstructed in the 1920s. The staccato of empty beam holes in the sheer cliff punches out the location of floors built in front of caves dug back into the living rock. Above shines a stone-relief sun as the spiral of life.

Behind these yawning holes in the rock are smoke-blackened connecting caves. Ventilation holes, niches, and toeholds provide a free-form cavernous apartment architecture of uncertain solids and voids in honeycombed tuff overlooking Tyuonyi Pueblo. Ladders allow tourists to peer into the darkness of prehistory.

Made luminous by the photographer, Puye's sheer cliff face of cindery tuff, with its filigree of lichen and stains, is contrasted by a foreground of rock debris and cactus and by a crown of rugged rocks. On that ancient face the inscribed tops of cave doorways appear like black sentinel ghosts. The horizontal rivet holes for vegas are enlivened by occasional sacred niches and practical ventilation holes.

Subtle detail emerges from the shadowed soft-edged openings in this richly textured print. Smoke-blackened caves at the top of the path at Puye play games positive and negative. Illusionary faces and imaginary kachina silhouettes in the powdery tuff dance with the futile pecking for beam pockets and ventilation holes.

The photographer deliberately framed a cave opening in a way that gives no hint of scale or interior, perhaps as a metaphor for the uncertainties "the ancient ones" faced. Fracture lines in the volcanic tuff provide a dynamic crystalline geometry to a doorway on the second level at Puye. The six-foot-high void facing the sun opens to the smoke-blackened darkness of the eight-foot-diameter stone space whose unique reverberatory tone seems visible on the outside.

Spooked faces, grotesque grottos, and ancient life forces seem to animate an uncertain cave entrance on the second level at Puye. Although the doorway opening is only three feet high, the interaction of volcanic stone and Anasazi carving has produced effects both hollowed and hallowed where no line divides human fantasies and the forces of nature.

Human architecture interlocks with nature's as a ladder ascends to Cave Kiva overlooking Tyuonyi. It is an invitation to continue the Anasazi mystery with a night experience amid dim fires and soft flute music with stories of coyotes and stars climaxed by the flintlike sparkles of striking together "lightning stone." The magical quartzite still comes from nearby White Rock.

The sheer cliff remains vertical and taut above the stub remains of apartment walls of Long House, to the west of Tyuonyi. The powerful meeting of canyon floor and natural wall is expressed in tonal gradations. This was the south-facing site of an eight-hundred-foot-long stone pueblo. Now the wall plaster of rooms and the sacred niches hang suspended in the etched rock sky.

A detail in the middle of the long wall of Long House seems to continue the forms of the previous photograph, but it shows a microcosm from its center. It is the ghost of a wall from one room symbolizing the whole of Long House with its 356 rooms. The sacred niche for a special object is no larger than seven inches long by three inches high. The remains of plaster and the remembered images of its end walls float in suspension above the eroded lower cliff and the remaining stubs of stone masonry walls.

Dramatic late-day lighting etches the grain of the cliff face at Long House in paired prints that master tactile description. The foreground of rubble and spindly cactus silhouettes the glowing rock fiber. The remaining traces of two- and three-story Anasazi pueblo constructions seem incidental to the dynamic order of crystallized nature. Each print is a chapter of prehistory.

Sinagua and Salado are prehistoric cultures with major Anasazi influences. Wupatki National Monument with several pueblo ruins is less than an hour north of Flagstaff. Slightly more than an hour south of Flagstaff are small national parks for Montezuma Well, Montezuma Castle, and Tuzigoot. The Salado sites are at Tonto National Monument overlooking the twentieth-century lake behind Roosevelt Dam, a three-hour drive from Phoenix on any of three routes.

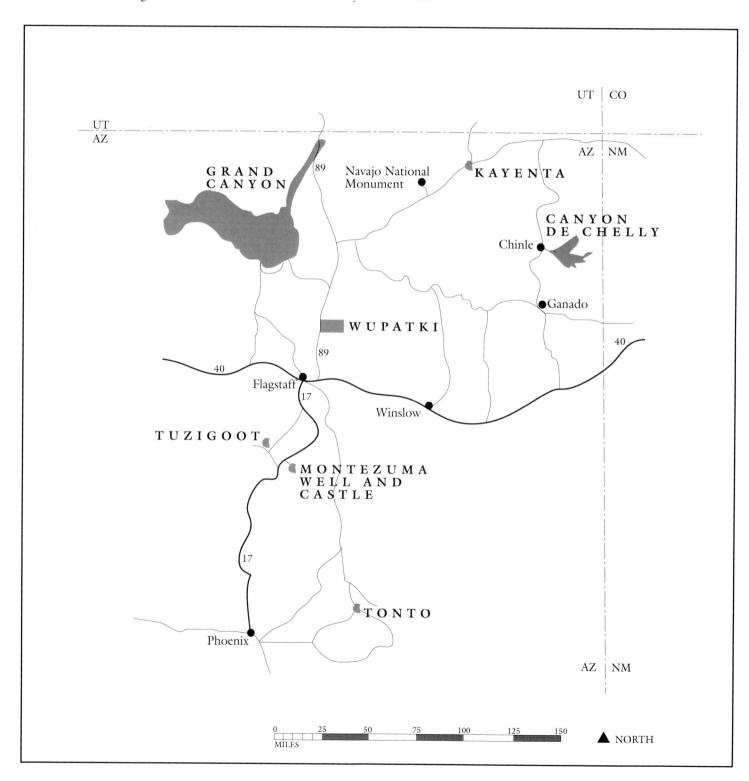

SINAGUA AND SALADO

The Sinagua were neighbors to the west of the Anasazi in prehistoric times. Named by the Spanish as the people "without water," the Sinagua had sparse settlements around A.D. 600 based on dry farming and hunting on rocky land near present-day Flagstaff, Arizona. During the winter of A.D. 1064–1065 a volcanic eruption formed Sunset Crater and destroyed their settlements. But the cultivation advantages of volcanic ash were soon discovered together with a climatic change that increased precipitation. This new agricultural opportunity resulted in a new settlement culture. Today the remains of those settlements are protected in the 35,000 acres of Wupatki National Monument.

Anasazi from the Kayenta region to the northeast are said to have joined the Sinagua together with Cohonina from the west to resettle near the volcanic fields northeast of the San Francisco Peaks. This amalgam of three diverse groups quickly developed a rich local culture in which the distinct architectural and planning prowess of the Anasazi is strongly visible in the remains. Wupatki, the Anasazi pueblo of more than one hundred rooms, also included an ovoid masonry ball court—the farthest north this prehistoric innovation from Central America is found.

Called Wupatki by the Hopi, the "tall house" of three stories was occupied between A.D. 1100 and 1225. But continuous drought beginning in 1215 forced abandonment. By the middle of the 1200s the Sinagua Anasazi had moved south into the well-watered Verde Valley. Anasazi traditions continued to dominate in the new pueblos of mixed peoples, such as at Tuzigoot and Montezuma Castle.

Both Tuzigoot and Montezuma Castle, although known as Sinagua sites, seem like classic Anasazi designs. The south-facing cliff dwelling at Montezuma Castle, with the apparent passive climatic control of its rock overhang, and the urbane citadel of Tuzigoot overlooking a fertile valley of A.D. 1300 are characteristic in their sensitive response to site. The T-shaped opening at Montezuma Castle is typical Anasazi. Perhaps only in the rhythmic curved walls at Montezuma Castle is there a new softness and sophistication to the disciplined designs found in the colder plateaus to the north.

Now national parks, Tuzigoot, Montezuma Castle, and Montezuma Well are easily accessible and popular. At Montezuma Well, a natural cup-shaped landform 1,750 feet in diameter continues to be fed by springs, an active oasis in a dry land. Montezuma Castle is widely known through publications, and almost a half million tourists visit each year. William Current's photographs of each site are comprehensive, direct, and typically sunny. They are classic renderings of classic sites.

Among the farthest south settlements where Anasazi influence is still visible are the fourteenth-century Salado villages that are now part of Tonto National Monument overlooking Lake Roosevelt. Here within and around stone cliffs and caves are the remains of three rock-constructed pueblos that synthesized Anasazi elements with traits from their southern and eastern neighbors. Here the plant and animal species of the arid high plateau overlap the most northern tolerance of hot desert species. The Anasazi now lived with the cholla and the saguaro cactus. They had dispersed themselves to be absorbed in the outer world.

The Salado story has only recently been deciphered. It began with alluvial farmers along the Salt River who moved up to the intermontane Tonto basin. These were Hohokam from the settlements around present-day Phoenix and farther south who colonized between A.D. 500 and 900. A number of significant cultural changes around A.D. 1150 imply the strong influx of outside influences that initiated a distinct Salado culture. Starting around A.D. 1300, coincident with the great migrations of the Anasazi, the Salado started building with stone and away from the low farmlands. The Anasazi T windows at the Tonto Cliff pueblos are only one indication of their potential cultural contributions. But there were no kivas, and the stone masonry was crude and without refinement. For the first time, the Salado built permanent settlements in high places overlooking valley below and sky and long vistas above.

The great Salado expansion of the fourteenth century resulted in hundreds of villages in the flats now covered by Lake Roosevelt as well as many settlements on high ground. At their peak there were tens of thousands living in the Tonto basin—a population that quickly outstripped the productive carrying capacity of nature. Evidence of malnutrition and shortened life expectations anticipated the disappearance of the Salado. By 1450 they had vanished.

Thus, the Salado had expanded their peaceful cooperative lifestyle beyond the resources of their place in nature. Did the Salado, whose great prosperity followed Anasazi immigrations, repeat the Anasazi pattern of abandonment? With the overpopulation of a peaceful people the choices are self-extermination or exile. Like the Hohokam at the same time or later, and the Anasazi before, the amalgam of Hohokam and Anasazi known as Salado also disappeared.

In the softly rolling Antelope Prairie of Wupatki National Monument, the pueblo ruin known as the Citadel architecturally completes a geologic promontory. But it appears to have no military agenda. The Anasazi visible love of the land and appreciation of distant views are summarized in this Sinagua construction that crests an airy symmetrical butte. In this serene image, Current captures with scale and pattern the essence of Anasazi habitation within the land.

The rhythms of layered stones with mud mortar come alive in the morning light through Current's lens. Emerging above the earth crust stratification of Sinagua Kaibab limestone is Lomaki, the Hopi name for "beautiful house." On the edge of a collapsed earth crack is a two- story microcosm of nine rooms that overlooks a macrocosm of unfathomable land. This Sinagua pueblo of A.D. 1192 could scan the parched horizons of dry grass and pastel ledges of the Painted Desert to the north.

Deliberate yet fragile human walls embrace raw bedrock at Lomaki. Below are the curved bins for food storage. Above is the continuity of massive dry masonry, where Kaibab limestone fragments are woven through with small Moenkopi sandstones. A vertical rift in the ponderous rock crust connects habitation with subterranean forces. Almost lost in the masonry wall above is a tiny square vent opening, the single geometric element of human perfection. The intertwining elements of Anasazi architecture—human geometries and immovable nature—are elegantly condensed.

The density of Sinagua pueblo design at Wupatki Ruin suggests the complex ordering of society in a structure of one hundred rooms. The urban form of "tall house" extends a natural stone ledge and eroded cliff face, interweaving nature with a roofless architectural textile. Cross walls and windows describe human dimensions. In Current's composition, an opening void against the sky creates tensions with blackened doorways.

Warmed by the morning light, the horizontally layered walls of the few rooms of Box Canyon Ruins are seen by the photographer as a diminutive echo of the natural order. The stable gross horizontal layers of Kaibab limestone provide an orderly base for delicate constructed stone walls with their intricate network of clay mortar joints, like the veins in a leaf.

The early fourteenth-century urban pueblo of Tuzigoot, Apache for "crooked water," is another version of a citadel, seen from the bottom of the hill. The web of stone walls extends the profile of a commanding hill near the river in the spacious Verde Valley. It is caught between a cloud-filled overarching sky and an earth of uncertain bounty. "The ancient ones" chose the high ground, centering the earth expanses of the Sinagua.

Cottonwoods in the Verde Valley thrive in the well-watered riparian habitat of a warmer desert climate. Above is an intense desert sky with the rising white cumulus clouds of spring, bounded by sleeping mountainous plateaus. Nature's corridor between the high arid country and the low hot deserts, the Verde Valley was a distinct and provident major niche in the ecologies of the harsh Southwest.

Rising 120 feet above the Verde River, Tuzigoot was a miniature mountain pueblo of more than one hundred rooms above the fertile floodplain. A rich layering of textures dramatizes the transitional crescendo from natural vegetation to dense urban pueblo to the scattered clouds, suggesting the interrelated continuities of the Anasazi world-view.

Montezuma Castle hangs like a swallow's nest in the crescent of the limestone cliff, above a curve in Beaver Creek. Mistakenly named after the Aztec emperor or refugees of his people from the Valley of Mexico, it is the most popular image of a cliff dwelling. Without visible stairs or ladders, and appearing to be complete and impenetrable, it is at once secure and protected. It is one of the great façades of all architecture, its overlapping and curved volumes organically merging within the rocky hollow.

With contrasting textures and masses, the wrinkled mud plaster of Montezuma Castle gives an illusion of great antiquity to this twelfth- and thirteenth-century vertical pueblo of some twenty rooms. But within the shadowed recess of a south-facing niche the pocked and eroded rock is much more ancient. The firm sweep of the multistoried Sinagua architecture continues the line of the cliff wall in a parallel but distinct order. Openings natural and human carry on their own dialogue. To the side a T-shaped doorway reveals the Anasazi presence.

In the cliff face below Montezuma Castle, voids in the eroded surface suggest past energies both natural and human. Hints of Sinagua stone walls and occasional beam holes are the traces of some of the ground-floor rooms abandoned around A.D. 1425. Time is the master. The imprints of human handiwork are absorbed by an omnipotent nature.

Like an X ray piercing the shadowy walls of Montezuma Well, the supra architecture of the earth's crust is revealed. Within its time-laden gargantuan layers and its fragments of the vegetative world, humans have found a sympathetic toehold. Sheltered under a massive limestone ledge, the Sinagua refined their cave with neat walls, a simple human gesture. This photograph of a prehistoric paradise resembles in its depth and density one of the prison series etchings by Piranesi (1720–1778), the great architectural artist.

Tapered stone walls cantilever from the ground like knife blades. The precision of masonry skills of the Lower Ruin at Tonto National Monument may celebrate the Anasazi contribution to the succeeding amalgam culture known as Salado. Sheltered below an overhanging cliff, the geometries of humans and nature resonate.

The Anasazi have long gone from the
lush luminous cactus landscape of
the Salado, yet in the blossoming
transitional ecologies toward the low
deserts, their understanding of a
correct and sympathetic human
place in the natural world persists.
Saguaro sentinels guard dwellings
sheltered not in nature but of nature.
Anasazi prehistoric culture was
simultaneously discrete and on high.

The rich play of palacelike architectural forms at Cliff Palace on Mesa Verde suggests creative variations within the egalitarian structure of mature Anasazi culture. Stepped cylindric kivas are hidden within retaining walls that embrace a huge boulder and guarded by a circular residential outlook tower. A powerful but diverse community is nestled within a sheltering cave roof.

THE LEGACY

In museums, the artifacts of the Anasazi may seem to be the artistic curiosities of a primitive and lost people. On the land, the memorable architectural artifacts of the Anasazi sing of the environmental harmonies of a wise culture in an inhospitable but grand place. Thus, beyond the scholarly significance of their archaeological middens and their artistic objects, is the treasure of their building remains. Theirs was not a stone architecture of commemorative tombs or religious monuments or hedonistic homes, but an architecture inventive and celebratory of community, indelibly rooted in an austere natural environment and creative of place.

The first three cultural signatures that distinguish the Anasazi from their neighbors and indeed identify them from all other peoples are architectural: the *kiva*, the round underground clan ceremonial spaces, derived from their ancient dwelling, the pit house; the *unit pueblo*, a cluster of two to twelve rooms for both storage and living, together with outdoor plaza or work space that includes the kiva; and, last, the *orientation* to the world, the kiva and plaza facing the south and to the southeast. Clearly, orientation was practiced as a spiritual conviction.

From the generous dimensions and careful construction of their kivas, we know that the Anasazi could have conceived and built a commodious domestic architecture to balance some ideas of comfort and convenience against their demanding natural environment. They chose instead to live primarily outdoors, in designed public space juxtaposed with nature, and to build for community. Their own private rooms were tiny retreats and storerooms. Thus, the Anasazi invented both community architecture and microclimatic design as a unity, as expressions of their love of the outdoors and of their belief in an ordered society. Orientation, although important to compensate for climate, was even more important as a physical commitment of cosmic connection. The wonder is in the quality of these built compositions of community, with refined stonework that sometimes resembles jewelry, that knowingly belong so completely to their chosen arid plateaus.

The cultural blossoming of the egalitarian Anasazi was of a nonmaterialistic society of nominal physical possessions. A peaceful and apparently nonhierarchical people, their most powerful censure was to ostracize, to refuse to talk or to allow participation by the

On the brow of Middle Mesa a reconstructed but unnamed Sinagua ruin memorializes the fusion of built and natural environments that characterize the place making of "the ancient ones." A citadellike construction against the clear sky, it commands a handsome landscape from a textured ridge. Below, a singular architectural element plays sentinel. Above, a tiny square window is sighted back toward Citadel ruin, a mile away.

offender. A nonspecialized people, each family or kin group made all of their own pottery, tools, and clothing. A largely outdoor people, they built magnificent architecture that included only the most modest interior living spaces.

Although greatly skilled in the naked-eye optics of surveying and astronomy, they refused rigid buildings or gridded cities and preferred a more subtle geometry of built form. Although they were sophisticated in their understanding of the geometry of the sun, their solar structures were metaphysical instruments of the spirit rather than primary thermal systems for the comfort of the flesh. Least understood is why these gentle people chose to live where we see desolate wastes and incredible vistas.

Among the immediate legacies of the Anasazi are their contributions to the genetic pool and to the beliefs and practices of the present-day Pueblos, including Acoma, Zuni, and Hopi. Just as each Anasazi pueblo unit thrived with a certain independent autonomy and thus individuality, so have their many successors developed independently. Each group has generated variations in their common story of origins and of the network of communications that maintain balance among the underworld, the earth's surface, and the upper level, the great sky bowl.

It is tempting and flattering to compare the architectural memories of the Anasazi with the worldly building accomplishments of other Stone Age peoples, when each entered their neolithic age of chipped stone tools and established the sedentary life of agriculture and domestic animals with permanent settlements. But this is ultimately a vain comparison. For the Anasazi it was not so much the material transformation of a marginally supportive place, for their high arid environment was forever tight in its providence, but in the aesthetic tuning to such a harsh place. It was never tamed, and that continues to be part of its powerful attraction. But within the natural diversity of food sources, water, and arable land, the Anasazi adaptively danced with their mother earth and won an enviable culture. It was a human artistic accomplishment of great and elegant economy.

Yet, within the ecological ethos, this state of human grace enigmatically soured. For reasons still not agreed, the paradise of the Anasazi became pathos.

The dilemma of their fall is among the Anasazi legacies. From a people who only wrote by building stone architecture, we must find our legacy among the stones. That is also among the themes of William Current's poignant photographic essays. Each image searches for recognizable order within the stillness of a dialectic nature. Each image invites human presence. Each image explores a natural environment both provident and malevolent, as the scene of built interventions. Each image articulates both the majesty and the mystery of natural environment as the stage for human sentience. Each image seeks place, for the Anasazi and for ourselves.

What is the latent force of prehistoric memories? Within the stillness of these selective historic photographs is the question of futures. The issue is not the Anasazi. They have had their stay and are gone. Their magnificent settlements will not be restored or revived. But in our own godlike presumptions about our own now global environment, which seems so much more richly provident than arid Anasazi plateau and canyon, how do we fare?

A beautiful interior doorway at Pueblo Bonito summarizes the classic accomplishments of a Stone Age architecture still intact but abandoned. The delicacy of finely fitted stones and the subtle line of the jambs of the opening are capped by the cylindrical stubs of the ceiling supports. This is a frontal and neutral view of static stability where all the forces of nature are synthesized in a knowing architecture.

Recommended Reading

Automobile Club of Southern California. *Guide to Indian Country*. Los
   Angeles and Tucson: Southwest Parks and Monuments Association,
   1989. The essential road map for motorists.
Cordell, Linda S. *Prehistory of the Southwest*. San Diego: Academic Press, 1984.
   A definitive introductory text in anthropology.
Current, William, and Vincent Scully. *Pueblo Architecture of the Southwest*.
   Austin: University of Texas Press, 1971. An earlier and shorter
   presentation of some of these photographs, long out of print.
Ebeling, Walter. *Handbook of the Indian Foods and Fibers of Arid America*.
   Berkeley: University of California Press, 1986. A mixed synthesis that
   identifies and systemizes many sources and puts the Anasazi into their
   domestic context.
Ferguson, William M., and Arthur H. Rohn. *Anasazi Ruins of the Southwest in
   Color*. Albuquerque: University of New Mexico Press, 1987. The most
   complete field guide and finders' reference, well illustrated.
Lister, Robert H., and Florence C. Lister. *Chaco Canyon: Archaeology and
   Archaeologists*. Albuquerque: University of New Mexico Press, 1981. A
   well-informed history of the canyon's exploration, excavation, and
   interpretation.
———. *Those Who Came Before*. Globe, Ariz.: Southwest Parks and
   Monuments Association, 1983. Beautifully illustrated and thorough
   introduction to southwestern archaeology in the national park system.
Smith, Jack E. *Anasazi Symposium 1981*. Mesa Verde National Park, Col.: Mesa
   Verde Museum Association, 1983. Proceedings of a conference with
   provocative papers from over thirty specialists, with an extensive
   bibliography.
Stuart, David E. *The Magic of Bandelier*. Santa Fe: Ancient City Press, 1989.
   One of the most comprehensive and best illustrated of single-site guides.
Viele, Catherine W. *Voices in the Canyon*. Tucson, Ariz.: Southwest Parks and
   Monuments Association, 1981. Handsomely illustrated and well informed
   about the Kayenta Anasazi.
Wormington, H. M. *Prehistoric Indians of the Southwest*. Denver: Denver
   Museum of Natural History, 1975. A standard popular reference first
   published in 1947.

Where Canyon de Chelly is at its widest, Navajo petroglyphs depict deer hunters on galloping horses pursuing their lively prey across the stone screen of Standing Rock, inspired by ancient Anasazi rock art.

INDEX